FINANCIAL ANALYSIS OF TAKEOVERS

FINANCIAL ANALYSIS
OF
TAKEOVERS

By
K. Ravi Sankar

ANMOL PUBLICATIONS PVT. LTD.
NEW DELHI - 110 002 (INDIA)

ANMOL PUBLICATIONS PVT. LTD.
4374/4B, Ansari Road, Daryaganj
New Delhi - 110 002
Ph.: 3261597, 3278000
Visit us at: www.anmolbooks.com

Financial Analysis of Takeovers

First Edition, 2003

ISBN 81-261-1437-1

PRINTED IN INDIA

Published by J.L. Kumar for Anmol Publications Pvt. Ltd., New Delhi - 110 002 and Printed at Mehra Offset Press, Delhi.

Dedicated to My Parents

Padmavati

&

Krishna Murthy

CONTENTS

PREFACE

In the recent times mergers and takeovers have generated considerable interest in the Indian corporate sector. This is because the topic encompasses such diverse areas as corporate ownership, growth and efficiency, monopoly and anti-competitive measures and so on. In India, with the on set of liberalization and economic restructuring the words like takeovers, mergers and strategic alliances have become buzz-words.

Takeovers are of different forms. Some of them involve straight takeover of one company by the other through the acquisition of shares and decision to operate the company as an independent entity. In some other cases, takeovers may be to the extent of capturing the controlling ownership in a company. A third variety in this is that sick companies are taken over by the healthy companies for the revival. For the purpose of this study, the third variety of the sample units have been, selected.

In India the research studies on takeovers are very few. Little is done from the point of view of establishing the fact that whether takeovers are able to produce results and thus they can be supported by the Government and others as a useful economic activity. More so in the context of turning around of sick units, takeover is considered to be an useful strategy. In this context, the present study aims at concentrating on the aspects relating to performance of the units being takeover by the new managements.

In this study an attempt is made to compare the

performance of firms before and after the takeover through the financial parameters like liquidity, leverage and profitability.

I am sincerely thankful to Prof. K.V. Rao, Nagarjuna University, Guntur for initiating me into research.

I am also thankful to the Authorities of IGNOU and BIFR for allowing me to pursue this study and supporting me in this work.

The support of my friends and family members is immense and they deserve a special thanks.

—K. Ravi Sankar

Chapter I

INTRODUCTION

In recent times mergers and takeovers have generated considerable interest amongst the laypersons as well as amongst those involved in this activity. This is because the topic encompasses such diverse areas as corporate ownership, growth and efficiency in the economy, monopoly and anti-competitive markets and so on. In India, with the onset of liberalisation and economic restructuring the words like 'takeovers', 'mergers' and 'strategic alliances' have become buzz-words. In the present study, the term 'takeover' is used in a broader sense to include all other terms such as merger, acquisition, and management change. When a company was taken over by another company the taking over company has two options. The first option is to merge both the companies into one and operate as a single entity, and the second is to operate the taken over company as an independent company, may be with changes in management and policies. The first option is known as 'merger' and the second as 'takeover' or 'change of management'. In the present study, though the word 'takeover' has been used in a broader sense, while selecting the sample units only the 'management change' cases have been selected.

This chapter has been divided into two parts. Part-I discusses the takeover phenomenon in general and the second part deals with the objectives, hypotheses and methodology of the study.

PART - I

1. INTRODUCTION

Mergers and takeovers have turned out to be a part of the strategies for expansion and growth of corporations. Expansion can be in the same field of operation called 'Horizontal Expansion' or in different fields called 'Conglomerate Expansion'. Where expansion results in up stream or down stream linkages to the existing field of operations it is called a 'Vertical Expansion'.

From the literature, it appears that the first type cases of mergers have occurred in the U.S. in late 1890s, in a non-merger context.

2. MERGERS AND ACQUISITIONS IN U.S.

Several merger and acquisition movements have occurred in the United States (Golbe and White, 1988)[1] and each was more or less dominated by a particular type of merger. All the movements occurred when the economy experienced sustained high rates of growth and coincided with particular developments in business environments (Weston, Chung and Hoag, 1996)[2]. The central issues of merger policy arose in a non-merger context. The year 1890 witnessed both passage of the Sherman Act and the publication of Alfred Marshall's Classic, *Principles of Economics* (Steiner, 1975)[3]. Golbe and White[4] classified the merger waves into four, as the wave of the turn of the century, in the late 1920s, in the late 1960s and in the 1980s. However, Weston, Chung and Hoag[5] have classified these waves into five as, (i) the wave of 1895-1904, (ii) the wave of 1922-1929, (iii) the wave of 1940-47, (iv) the wave of 1960s and (v) the wave after 1980s.

The first merger movement occurred between the period 1895-1904. This movement consisted mainly of horizontal mergers, which resulted in high concentration in many industries. The period was one of rapid expansion. The movement reached its peak in 1899 and almost ended in 1903, when a severe economic recession set in. This merger movement was accompanied by major changes in economic infrastructure and production technologies by the turn of the century (Markham[6], 1955, p. 156; Salter and Weinhold[7] 1980, p.7).

The second wave of mergers, as in the first merger movement, also began with an upturn in business activity in 1922 and ended with the onset of a severe economic slowdown in 1929.

Many combinations in this period occurred outside the previously consolidated heavy manufacturing industries. The public utilities and banking industries were among the most active groups. This period witnessed a transformation of a near-monopoly to an oligopoly (Stingler, 1950)[8]. A large portion of mergers in the 1920s represented product extension mergers. Both Markham[9] and Stocking[10] (1955) emphasised major developments in transport, communication and merchandising as the motivational factors of these mergers.

The third movement, which occurred during 1940 and 1947, was much smaller than the earlier ones and there were no pervasive motives for this merger movement other than the conventional ones. However, Government's regulation and tax policies were pointed out by some economists as having motivated mergers in this period (Stingler[11], 1951;Butters, Lintner and Cary[12] (1951)).

The fourth wave of mergers came in 1960s and the focus of these mergers shifted from the horizontal and vertical types to conglomerate type. Merger activity reached its peak during the three-year period of 1967 through 1969. This period was also one of a booming economy. The number of mergers declined sharply as the general economic activity slowed down after 1969. Most of the mergers in this period were small-or medium-sized firms that adopted a diversification strategy into business activities outside their traditional areas of interest. In this period, the largest single category of firms is from Aerospace industry.

Following the recession in 1974-1975, the U.S. economy entered a long period of expansion, during which takeovers trended upward. Since 1976, mergers and acquisitions have been concentrated in such service industries as commercial and investment banking, finance, insurance, wholesale, retail, broadcasting and health care, and in natural resource areas. This trend reflected the increasing importance of these industries in the U.S. economy. Another characteristic of the current wave of merger activity is that divestitures became a substantial portion of acquisition activity. Through out the 1980s, they have represented over 35 per cent of all mergers and acquisition transactions.

To sum up, it may be concluded that during 1920s vertical and horizontal mergers were common and in 1960s and 1970s conglomerate mergers were popular. However, the percentage of conglomerates decreased in 1980s and the divestitures have been occurring. Thus, each of the merger waves of U.S. is following a particular method of merger and acquisition activity.

3. MERGER TRENDS IN U.K.

The degree of concentration in British Industry has increased considerably since the World War II at the aggregate and market levels. The history of the takeovers in the U.K. can be studied in 5 phases[13]. They are: (1) Before 1939 (2) Between 1939-45, (3) Between 1945-65 (4) Between 1965-73, (5) 1973 Onwards.

Before 1939

Prior to 1939, the British Industry had many features of perfect competition, such as the existence of many producers with few firms able to dominate the market. Though, during the First World War some associations were formed, the competition could not be reduced. The Government policy at that time was to encourage free trade and intervene where the markets seemed to react slowly. The great depression of 1929-

31, brought changes in the attitude of the Government and the British Industry underwent some restructuring and formed trade associations and cartels. However, all these efforts were interrupted by the advent of the Second World War.

Between 1939-45

During this period, trade associations and cartels continued to dominate, and the competitive environment, prevalent in the early part of the century, was destroyed. Owing to the outbreak of the Second World War, the Government had to have a high degree of control on the trade and industry and the formation of associations and cartels facilitated the Governmental efforts. The Government also encouraged the formation of cartels during this period. As the War came to an end, the Government, wanted to bring back the competitive environment into the economy but the industry wanted to maintain the existing structure. In addition to this, the traditional industry of Britain had old or obsolete plant, which could not compete successfully with foreign competition. The employment policy white paper issued in 1944 suggested that the trade associations should play a useful role in improving efficiency and the mergers to be encouraged to take advantage of economies of scale. During this period there were attempts to regulate monopolies and restrictive practices.

Between 1945-65

During this period, most of the legislative work relating to the regulation of cartels, monopolies and restrictive practices has been brought out. In 1948, the Monopolies and Restrictive Practices (Inquiry and Control) Act gave rise to the constitution of the Monopolies and Restrictive Practices Commission. Though the Commission was not successful, in performing its job, it became obvious that a great many malpractices were prevalent in the British Industry. To check these malpractices, the Government brought out the Restrictive Trade Practices Act in 1956. This Act had a dramatic impact on restrictive practices and cartels. On the surface, the Act had been very successful.

However, many of the formal agreements registered may have been replaced by 'gentlemen's agreements' or even by mergers.

Between 1965-73

In 1965, the Monopolies Commission was reorganized and strengthened by the Monopolies and Mergers Act. With this Act, the Commission was given the power to investigate mergers where the assets involved exceeded 5 million pounds. During this period, competition increased not only because of the efforts of the Government but also because of increase in international trade. To compete successfully at an international level, it became inevitable that some British Companies would need to merge to gain from economies of large-scale production and became as large as some of their rivals in Europe and the U.S. Government also encouraged mergers in particular sectors of the economy.

1973 Onwards

In 1973, the Fair Trading Act was passed requiring the Director General of Fair Trading to keep the commercial activities relating to goods and services under constant review. It is the responsibility of the Director General to scrutinize all mergers. In addition to this Act, anti-competition provisions were introduced into the Companies Act, 1980.

4. INDIAN SCENARIO

In India, the takeover activity was on a low key till 1970s. Discussions were generally conducted across the board and negotiated settlements reached among the parties concerned, but for a few rare cases. When Swaraj Paul launched the famous raids on DCM Ltd. and Escorts Ltd. in the early 1980s, the role of Financial Institutions was brought under considerable scrutiny. Swaraj Paul's bids were a forerunner in this respect and they constituted a watershed in the corporate history of the country. With the Swaraj Paul's episode shareholders began to matter in a more real sense to the controlling interest and things like Earnings Per Share, Price Earnings Ratio, market price of share were given attention to. This episode also gave rise to a whole new trend of another sort and a group of financially strong individuals entered the takeover game to make their presence felt as industrialists. Some of the big names in this takeover game in the early days were Ram Prasad Goenka, M.R. Chhabria, Sudarshan Birla, Srichand Hinduja, Vijay Mallya and Dhirubhai Ambani. However, in 1990s many of these continued to be in this game and some new names like Hindusthan Lever Ltd., Arvind Group, Eicher Group, Rajarathinam, Ajay Piramal got added to this list. The takeover of the Shaw Wallace by M.R. Chhabria and repeated attempts of Reliance Industries to takeover L & T Ltd., are some of the historical cases of the Indian takeover phenomenon.

If the period between 1970s and early 80s is considered as the first wave of takeover movement in India, the wave during the period 1988 and 92 could be considered as the second movement. During this period there were about 121 takeovers and mergers which were successfully carried out and 37 takeover bids which were found unsuccessful. This wave occurred mainly owing to the liberalisation of industrial licensing. The difference between the first and second takeover wave was that the game was no longer dominated by the single players and the firms of divergent character such as small and big, having low profile and high profile and of Indian and foreign origin were participating in the game.

The third wave started in the year 1992 with liberalisation policies adopted by the then Government. Necessary changes were incorporated in concerned legislations including Foreign Exchange Regulation Act (FERA), the Monopolies and Restrictive Trade Practices Act (MRTP Act) and the Industries (Development and Regulation) Act (IDA). As a result of this, the firms have substituted their growth plans with the takeover strategies. This is because the benefits of taking over a company are lucrative enough to make this strategy preferable to organic growth. The Privatisation Policy of the Government also encouraged the takeover activity during this period. After carefully guarding the enterprises it floated, the Government is now selling parts of those very enterprises. Allwyn Ltd., HMT Ltd. and Ahemedabad Electricity Company are the examples of this type.

With the MRTP Act and the FERA no longer constraints, a number of multi-national corporations (MNCs) are merging their Indian subsidiaries. The Brooke Bond India and Lipton India, ABB and GEC Alsthom are some of the examples for this. Wherever no Indian subsidiaries are available, the MNCs are buying the suitable Indian companies and entering the Indian market through them. Coco Cola's tie-up with Parle Exports is an example of this. As a result of the increased presence of MNCs in Indian Market, even the Indian companies felt the need to restructure their own businesses. In this process the companies are identifying their core competencies that will help them to cope with tomorrow and shedding their unrelated business and consolidating their chosen areas of operation. While the shedding implies that most groups have companies to sell, the consolidation implies that the companies must buy up their competitors. Both of these activities are triggering a chain-reaction of takeovers across the country. The classic example for this is the merger between Tata Oil Mills Company Ltd. and Hindusthan Lever Ltd.

Another interesting trend during this period is that there are conglomerates also. People like Rajarathinam have gone on takeover spree and purchased all kinds of companies without having any relation to one another.

As a result of all the above changes, even the sick units, are finding many buyers and the Financial Institutions (F.I.s) are able to sell these sick units easily. Even the Board for Industrial and Financial Reconstruction (BIFR) is keen that the sick companies be acquired quickly, and thereby, has become a facilitator of the takeover deals.

It was felt that the takeover activity may take place in future in areas like: Cement, Tyres, Consumer Durables, Consumer

Non-Durables, Financial Services, Machine Tools, Paper and Power Generation.

5. MOTIVES BEHIND THE TAKEOVERS

Any acquisition takes place with a number of motivations culminating in a positive synergy (2+2 = 5 relationship). This means that the performance of the combined company is more than the sum of the performance of erstwhile two independent companies. Let us, now, examine the motives behind the takeover.

A study conducted in the U.S.A., identified 12 motives that promote merger and acquisition activity. They are given below in the order of their priority.

1. Taking advantage of awareness that a company is undervalued.
2. Achieving growth more rapidly than by internal effort.
3. Satisfying market demand for additional product/services.
4. Avoiding risks of internal start-ups of expansion.
5. Increasing earnings per share.
6. Reducing dependence on a single product/service.
7. Acquiring market share or position.
8. Offsetting seasonal or cyclical fluctuations in the present business.
9. Enhancing the power and prestige of the Owner, CEO, or Management.
10. Increasing utilisation of present resources, eg., physical plant and individual skills.
11. Acquiring outstanding Management or Technical Personnel.
12. Opening new markets for present products/services.

A survey, conducted in 1955, by the U.S. Federal Trade Commission ,to find out why companies choose the merger and acquisition route, listed seven major benefits of acquisition for the acquiring company. They are:

1. Gaining additional capacity to supply to a market already being serviced by the acquirer.
2. Gaining extended product lines.
3. Achieving diversification of product base.
4. Gaining facilities to produce goods purchased earlier.
5. Gaining facilities to process or distribute goods sold earlier.
6. Gaining access to additional markets.
7. Other advantages such as empty plants, control of patents, etc.

In India, the merger and takeover phenomenon in the past is largely one of the sick units being taken over by healthy ones. This is because of the reason that Sec. 72A of the Income Tax Act, 1961, provides for the carry forward of losses. The advantage that the merging corporations get is that the book losses of the sick corporation get written off against the future profits, thus saving the profitable corporations some tax outflow.

6. LEGAL FRAMEWORK

Mergers and takeovers are generally seen in Public Policy as activities, which, if left uncontrolled, can lead to negation of Public interests. As a result, these activities are controlled through various Statutes and Codes of Conduct. Some of the contentious issues that emphasise the need for evolving a Takeover Code are discussed below.

Sec.s 111 and 390 to 396 A of the Companies Act, 1956, govern mergers and acquisitions. Similarly Sections 19, 26 and 29 of the erstwhile FERA related to transfer of shares. Where one of the transacting parties is a Non-Resident Indian, the Act prohibits the transaction except with the sanction of the Reserve Bank of India (R.B.I.). Sec.s 30(A) to 30(F) of the MRTP Act pertain to transfer of shares relating to dominant undertakings as defined in the Act. Further, Sec. 22 (A) of the Securities Contract (Regulation) Act, 1956, deals with the transfer of shares. Clauses 40 (A) and 40 (B) of the Stock Exchange Listing Agreement Form also lay down the rules in case of takeover bids.

In spite of all the above Regulations and Laws, there are lots of unfair things and complaints against the way takeovers are carried out. In some takeovers, companies are accused of charges of inside information, clandestine transactions and inadequate disclosure of intent. In some others, corporate raiders complained about misleading information, insider trading and political clout. With present liberalisation and globalisation process, it is very likely that merger and acquisition activity is now going to boom further. The old rules would not be able to govern this boom in the best interest of the Public. To meet this kind of situation, the Securities and Exchange Board of India (SEBI) has created a legal framework for the newly-liberalised market for mergers and acquisitions. The SEBI has mooted a Takeover Code that insures transparency in merger and acquisition deals.

7. TAKEOVER AS A STRATEGY OF TURNAROUND

Among the several ways of turning around a sick company, Management change is one of the popular ways. In this method, a healthy company buys a sick company. Then, the question arises, why a healthy company should buy a sick company. There could be a variety of reasons. For instance, the acquisition may strengthen its own position where it has an established product line, or the taking over company may wish to diversify into another related or unrelated areas. The main attraction is that when the company, which is being taken over, is sick, it can be purchased at a lesser price than its real value. Some countries give tax incentives when a sick company is taken over.

All these factors motivate a healthy company to buy a sick company.

On the other hand, a sick company agrees for takeover, as there would not be any other alternative than liquidating. Naturally, companies would like to accept takeover than going for winding-up. Sometimes, even the taking over company may offer better price than the prevailing market price, thus making the takeover attractive. Once the takeover is completed, the taking over company brings fresh managerial talent and additional resources in the process of turning the company around.

8. THE BIFR AND TAKEOVERS

In India, the takeover of sick units is processed through the BIFR. Under Sick Industrial Companies Act (SICA), 1985, it is mandatory for a sick unit to report to the BIFR for its winding-up or rehabilitation. As far as possible, the BIFR tries to rehabilitate a sick unit rather than winding it up.

The Principal Objectives of the BIFR are:

(a) to evaluate the techno - economic viability of sick units with a view to rehabilitate or close them down

(b) to stop continued drain of public and private resources

(c) to protect employment, as far as practicable

The BIFR has many ways to rehabilitate a sick unit like leasing or selling a division of the sick unit or to merge with a healthy unit, or to change the management with a new management and so on. Among these measures, merger or change of management are proved to be a better way of turning around a sick unit. Merger enables healthy units with large taxable profits to gain by setting off losses of the taken over units against their tax liabilities. Many companies are taking over sick units, in order to gain from synergy or vertical integration or diversification. Especially where large sick units are involved, the merger or takeover through the BIFR schemes should be the better route of revival, as this route is less cumbersome and faster than the Courts.

PART-II

9. STATEMENT OF THE PROBLEM

Takeover phenomenon, which swept the West during the sixties and seventies, has come down to India during late eighties and terms such as mergers, acquisitions and takeovers have turned out to be buzz words today. With the adoption of liberalisation policies in the Indian economy in late eighties, the Indian corporate sector too has started experiencing takeover activity.

The first wave of takeover activity in India can be said to have taken place between 1977 and 1985. During this period, the number of takeovers was few. With the liberalisation of provisions in the Industries (Development and Regulation) Act, 1951 and Monopolies and Restrictive Trade Practices Act, 1969, the second phase of takeover activity started in 1988, and there occurred 121 mergers and acquisitions during 1988-92. There has been a significant spurt in takeover activity since 1992. The game of takeover is now played by units of divergent character such as small and big, having low profile and high profile and of Indian and Foreign origin. As per the data available, it is estimated that about 1,000 mergers and takeovers have occurred between 1992 and 1995.

Though the takeover phenomenon is sweeping across India in the 90's, there are no scientific studies done on the performance evaluation of the takeover units except few newspaper writings. Though a few researchers have concentrated on the takeover activity, they focused much on the motives and the capital market related matters. Little is done from the point of view of establishing the fact that whether takeovers are able to produce results and thus the Government and others can support them as a useful economic activity. More so in the context of turning around of sick units, takeover is considered to be an useful strategy. In this context, the present study aims to concentrate on the aspects relating to performance of the units being taken over by the new management. Sample selection is made from only sick companies for the sole reason that these changes in these units can be clearly identified. Hence, the study is based on the Board for Industrial and Financial Reconstruction (BIFR) cases, for the selection of the sample, which have undergone management change (takeover) as a strategy for the revival (turnaround).

Under the Sick Industrial Companies Act, 1985, it is mandatory for a sick unit to report to the BIFR for its winding-up or for rehabilitation. As far as possible, the BIFR tries to rehabilitate a sick unit rather than winding it up. Generally, rehabilitation is done in the following ways:

1. Financial reconstruction of the company.
2. The amalgamation of the sick company with any other company or any other company with the sick company.
3. Sale or lease of a part or whole of any industrial unit of the sick company.
4. Proper management of the sick industrial company by change in or takeover of management of the sick company.

The BIFR after considering all the factors and feelings of all the stakeholders, may sanction any one of the above methods in order to turn the company around.

For the present study, it is proposed to study the companies, which have been recommended by the BIFR for change of management or takeover, by a new management as a turnaround strategy. The study includes a comparison of the performance of these sick units during the pre and post-takeover periods from the points of view of Liquidity, Leverage and Profitability.

10. OBJECTIVES OF THE STUDY

The main objective of the present study is to verify whether the takeover had turned the companies around or not. More specifically, the study deals with the following:

1. To probe into whether the liquidity of the companies has improved with the takeover.

2. To study the effect of leverage on liquidity and on profitability and its changes over the study period.
3. To examine whether the takeover is leading the companies from losses to profits, as expected with the takeover.
4. To verify whether the taking over companies with better and proven management skills are able to bring about better and faster results.
5. To understand whether the companies selected for study are able to expand their activities after the takeover.

11. HYPOTHESES

In the light of the objectives described above, the following hypotheses are intended to be tested for their acceptance or non-acceptance:

1. The company should turnaround and achieve better liquidity, particularly the short-term liquidity, after the takeover.
2. The capital structure of the taken over company should change in such a way that it should result in better solvency, liquidity and profitability.
3. When a company has been taken over by the new management, the company should turnaround and the profitability should improve.
4. The companies that were taken over by the better-known industrial groups, who have proven abilities of managing, shall turnaround faster than those that were taken over by the relatively lesser-known groups or individuals.
5. When a takeover of a sick unit takes place, the taken over company with the support of the taking over company shall try to expand or modernize their business activities in the process of their turning around.

12. SURVEY OF LITERATURE

The issues pertaining to liquidations, mergers, takeovers, acquisitions and reorganisations have attracted the attention of the researchers from the beginning of the development of finance literature. The early writings in finance are invariably included the discussions on the above issues. The writings of Greene[14] (1897), Meade[15] (1910) and Dewing[16] (1914) come under this category. While tracing the evolution of Finance, the authors including James C. Van Horne has emphasized the large number of consolidations during the turn of century and the depression of thirties as the motivators of these discussions on takeovers. However, almost all these discussions centered around the issue of raising funds for these takeovers. This trend continued upto 1950s. In 1950s authors like Markham[17] (1955), Stocking[18] (1955), Stingler[19] (1950), Butters, Lintner and Cary[20] (1951) have started studying with a specific focus on takeovers and the various issues involved in the takeovers. However, it appears that the focus of research on studying the financial gains started in late 1960s with the writings of Eamon Kelly[21] (1967) and Samuel Reid[22] (1968). Statistical research on takeovers has taken two main forms: (a) the analysis of profit, sales, employment and other data generated by one or both of the merging enterprises; and (b) the analysis of external data, such as stock market reactions to the events occurring at the time of takeover and its aftermath. Some of the studies in the first category are Kelly[23] (1967), Hogarty[24] (1970), Franks[25] et al., and so on, and in the second category are Gort[26] (1962), Halpern[27] (1973), Gagnon[28] (1982) and so on. However, few researchers like Weston and Mansinghka[29], Baruch Lev and Gershon Mandelkar[30] (1972) have studied the takeovers from both the above perspectives.

Studies of mergers occurring in the period from 1955 to 1965, tended to produce a uniform picture of merger targets as relatively unprofitable, sluggish, over-liquid firms, often with a history of static or declining earnings and dividends. On the other hand these studies also found the acquiring firms to be somewhat above average in profitability, with a tradition of retaining and reinvesting profits rather than paying large dividends and with having less than an average liquidity. In general, these were the findings of Hayes and Taussing[31] (1967) and of Ajit Singh[32] (1971). This kind of findings opened the possibility that many merger targets were potentially failing firms and to view mergers as an efficient alternative of avoiding bankruptcy. Boyle[33] (1970) explored and largely exploded this possibility. He studied 698 of the 1,275 acquired firms in large acquisitions over the period 1948-68 for which complete financial data were available for the five years preceding acquisition. His study effectively refuted the hypothesis of merger as a response to impending bankruptcy. This finding has received repeated support from other samples.

The FTC Report[34] (1970), found that the great majority of the target companies acquired by the nine leading conglomerate acquirers, earned profits in the period before acquisition, even though they were somewhat below average for their industries.

Denis Binder[35] (1973) dealing with a sample, biased by the self-selection of targets as those that have contended the attempt to acquire them, found the target companies to be generally profitable through out the decade.

Brain Hindley[36] (1973) sheds a different, but not contradictory light on this question as a by-product of an asset to explore the hypothesis that mergers are motivated by the profit opportunities arising from takeovers of inefficiently run firms. His principal finding is that an index of the ineffectiveness of the incumbent management was very much higher for the targets than for controls, and thus provided support for the hypothesis that mergers are transactions in the market for corporate control.

Another area where the research focused was on how the acquiring firms fared after the merger. Eamon Kelly's[37] (1967) study deals with 21 matched pairs of firms from the population of the 500 largest manufacturing and 50 largest merchandising firms over the period 1946-60. Kelly studied the profits to shareholders of the two firms as judged by the market performance of the stocks of the companies comparing the five pre-merger and five post-merger years. He found no significant pattern of differences in the success of the two groups measured by this standard. Merging firms grew faster and had high PE ratio than their non-merging counterparts, but did not translate this into more rapidly increasing stock prices over the period. Kelly concluded that the acquiring firms apparently paid too high a premium for the extra sales they acquired.

Samuel Reid[38], (1968) in a study looked at 478 of the 500 largest firms of 1961 and related the intensity of merger activity to two sets of variables: growth variables, and profit to shareholders variables. His major findings are that the more intensive the level of merger activity is the relatively better is the performance of the growth variables and relatively worse the performance of the profit variables.

Thomas Hogarty[39] studied 43 heavily merging firms over the period 1953-64. As a control for each such firm he used the average firm of the industry of the acquirer. His performance measures relied both on the prices of stocks and also on dividend policies, thus correcting an unfortunate oversight in Kelly's measures. Hogarty, found that most of these firms did not generate stock market performance for their stockholders that was better than the average firm of their industry, and many performed worse. There was, however, great variance, and a few were enormously successful.

Using the Hogarty's sample, Gort and Hogarty[40] (1970) found that the buyers as a whole lost and sellers gained, with the net transaction providing approximately zero-sum. Thus unless managers were risk prone, they concluded, mergers of this period were founded on the unjustified optimism of the acquiring firms. Weston and Mansinghka compared 63 conglomerate companies with two control groups randomly selected from among the Fortune 500 industrials and 250 non-industrials. Their data covered the periods 1958-68 and 1960-68. They have reached three principal conclusions:

1. The greater than average relative growth of acquirers reflected merger activity rather than greater internal

growth. This greater growth, contrary to earlier studies, extended to stock prices. Earlier studies, they believe, suffered from a too-early termination date.

2. To the extent that earnings performance on net worth of conglomerates was somewhat higher than for the control of groups, this resulted from increased use of debt financing. But the actual differences in earnings were small.

3. The earnings of the conglomerates at the start of the period were lower than those of the controls but by 1968 they had become not significantly different.

This study was of primary importance as it suggests the conglomerates' economic success was in raising the profitability of firms with depressed earnings to the average for industry generally. Baruch Lev and Gershon Mandelker[41] (1972), studied 69 matched pairs of firms covering the period of 1952-63. Their study was similar in many ways to the Kelly study, although more fully and carefully done. Their focus, however, was on major mergers rather than on heavily merging firms. Each acquiring firm in a major merger was matched with a firm from its own four-digit industry by asset size. Profits and other measures were computed for the five years prior to merger and for the five subsequent years. Both levels and dispersion of selected measures of performance were studied. Lev and Mandelkar found that acquiring firms were somewhat more profitable than their non-merging partners, in terms of subsequent stock market performance. Like Weston and Mansinghka, they found that if 'growth' is to mean acquisition of assets by any means, merging firms tended to grow faster, but that if growth is defined to be post-merger internal growth, they tended to grow more slowly.

Turning to the position prevailing in India, the literature on this subject is very scanty. Excepting some casual writings here and there, no serious attempt has been made to study various issues involved in the takeover activity. Perhaps this is because of the fact that the phenomenon itself, is of recent origin, particularly of 1970s.

An early attempt in this regard was made by V.S. Keveri[42] (1986). He has studied the financial performance of a sample of nine sick units and focused on their expectations from the mergers. He hypothesised that the performance of the sick company should improve after the takeover and the same can not be achieved if the takeover has not taken place. Though he has attempted to study the cases of nine companies, the study could not yield conclusions for generalising the phenomenon.

Another study made by Malay K. Roy[43] (1989) attempted to study takeovers from a corporate finance approach. Broadly the study considers different methods of valuation of shares in the context of takeovers, mode of financing an acquisition and its impact on capital structure and riskiness of the firm, impact of acquisition on the EPS and impact of mergers on share prices. However, the cases included in the study are not uniform and he tried to depend much on secondary data. N. Ashok Kumar and Rajas Parchure[44] (1990) had tried to deal with various issues of takeovers like accounting and finance, legal, and public policy. This study is more of theoretical in nature. This has largely been due to the paucity of published case material and the confidentiality associated with this activity.

Besides the above studies there are some journalistic writings in business magazines but they may not serve any purpose in the present context. Therefore, they are not reviewed here. The journals published by the professional bodies like the Institute of Cost and Works Accountants of India and the Chartered Accounts of India also carried some writings. Though these writings do not have much research inputs, they cover various issues involved in takeovers. Mostly these writings deal with legal and accounting aspects.

Against this background, the present study aims at concentrating on the performance of the taken over units before and after the takeover, with a particular emphasis on whether there is any improvement after the takeover.

13. SCOPE OF THE STUDY

Takeovers are of different forms. Some of them involve

straight takeover of one company by the other through the acquisition of shares and deciding to operate the company as an independent entity. In some other cases, takeover may be to the extent of capturing the controlling ownership in a company. A third variety in this is that sick companies are taken over by the healthy companies for their revival. For the purpose of this study, the third variety of the sample units have been selected from the records of the BIFR.

Therefore, the selected units were sick as per the definition of the Sick Industrial Companies Act, 1985.

The SICA provides for the revival of a sick company in the following two ways:

1. By giving a reasonable time, if it is practicable for a sick company to make its net worth exceed the accumulated losses under Sec.17, and
2. By sanctioning a rehabilitation scheme under Sec. 18.

A rehabilitation scheme, under the second alternative may provide any one or more of the following measures:

(a) Financial reconstruction of the sick company.

(b) Amalgamation of the sick company with any other company.

(c) Sale or lease of a part or whole of any industrial undertaking of the sick company.

(d) Rationalisation of managerial personnel, supervisory staff and workmen in accordance with the relevant laws.

(e) Proper management of the sick company by change in the management of the sick company.

Among the alternatives listed above, the present study focuses its attention on the 'change in management' as a strategy of rehabilitation. In other words, this study attempts to study the successfulness or otherwise of the takeover as a strategy of turnaround.

Further takeover phenomenon can be analysed from various aspects like economic, social, legal and public policy. The present study aims to analyse the implications of takeover from the financial point of view. This study is mostly quantitative in nature and the above qualitative aspects are outside the purview of this study.

14. METHODOLOGY

14.1. Selection of the Sample Units

The selection of the sample units has been done basing on the records compiled by the BIFR. According to the BIFR data, there were 38 cases, which have been sanctioned management change (takeover) as a revival strategy upto 31st March,1996. This list includes all those takeover cases that were disposed by the BIFR between October 1989 and May 1995. The selection of sample units is made as per the following procedure:

1. At the first stage, all the cases that were disposed off by the BIFR upto the end of 1993 were considered. This list comprised 24 cases.

2. At the second stage, an analysis of the operating agencies of the above 24 units had been done. From the analysis, we came to know that the Industrial Credit and Investment Corporation of India (ICICI) has acted as an operating agency for seven units, the erstwhile Industrial Reconstruction Bank of India (IRBI) for five units, the Industrial Finance Corporation of India (IFCI) for three units, the Industrial Development Bank of India (IDBI) and the Canara Bank for two units each, and the Central Bank of India, the Punjab National Bank and the State Bank of India for one unit each. No operating agency had been mentioned in case of the remaining two units. Keeping aside those organisations that acted as operating agencies for one or two units, we have selected the remaining three organisations, thus leaving the ICICI,

the IRBI and the IFCI with a total of 15 units. Of these 15 units, two units have not started implementing the revival scheme for various reasons like court cases or differences between Financial Institutions and the Management of the companies thus reducing the sample size to 13 units.

When the researcher approached these 13 units for data, some companies could not be contacted as the factory premises were closed implying that the unit has been closed, and some have not responded positively in spite of our repeated requests. As a result, we were left with a sample of 8 cases, which is one third of the cases of takeover, which have been settled upto 1993 by the BIFR. The following is the list of sample cases included in the study:

1. Dempo Dairy Industries Ltd., Bangalore
2. Industrial Chemicals and Monomers Ltd. (ICML), Sankarnagar (T.N.)
3. Amar Dye-Chem Ltd., Bombay
4. Bokiyu Tanneries Ltd., New Delhi
5. India Precision Bearings Manufacturers Ltd. (formerly, Kunal Machinery), Madras
6. Coromandal Pharmaceuticals Ltd., Hyderabad
7. Mico Farm Chemicals Ltd., Madras, and
8. Sivamani Spinning and Weaving Mills Ltd., Selam (T.N.)

All the above 8 cases were registered with the BIFR during the years 1987 and 1988 and they belong to different industries like electrical, food processing, textile and chemicals. The accumulated loss of these units varied between the highest of Rs.1,658.09 lakh in case of Amar Dye-Chem and the lowest of Rs. 90.19 lakh in case of Sivamani Spinning. As per the scheme of sanction, most of these companies have to make their net worth positive before 1994-95.

14.2. Sources of Data

The main source of data for this study has been the official records and publications of the BIFR. This is supplemented with the information compiled from annual reports of the selected companies, the Official Stock Exchange Directory of Bombay Stock Exchange and the other secondary data published in the books, journals and newspapers. In addition to this, the researcher also visited the units and held discussions with the executives from time to time during the course of study.

14.3. Analysis of Data

Since the main objective of the study is to examine whether the takeover has helped the sample units to improve their position, data have been compiled and analysed with a view to draw conclusions about the performance of these units before and after the takeover. In this study the actual years have been coded as Y_o, Y_{-1}, Y_4 and so on, as they do not have any relevance. The relevant things are the year of takeover, the years before the takeover and the years after the takeover, The year of takeover is taken as Y_o and the years prior to the takeover are labeled as Y_{-4}, Y_{-3}, Y_{-2}, Y_{-1} and the years after takeover are identified as Y_1, Y_2, Y_3 and so on. In addition to this, the latest year for which accounting information has been indicated with Y_n in specifying the general sequence. In many cases Y_n has been 1995-96.

While making comparison of the position obtained prior to takeover and after, heavy reliance is made on ratio analysis. Appropriate ratios as suggested in the literature are computed. Depending upon the nature of the data and need of the study statistical tools like proportions and percentages, and decomposition analysis have been used in the study.

14.4. Limitations of the Data:

The following are the limitations faced during the study:

1. Since the study is mainly financial in nature, data presented in the annual reports are taken as the base

for analysis. The limitations that might be applicable to such data also apply to the present study.

2. In case of Coromandal Pharma the data for the years Y_1, Y_2, Y_3 and Y_4 are not available for 12 months. Years Y_1 and Y_2 have 15 months data, year Y_3 has 18 months data and on the contrary year Y_4 has 8 months data. However, while making analysis, the data for these years have either reduced or inflated, as the case may be, to 12 months to maintain uniformity.

3. The data for Sivamani Spinning was not available for the years Y_{-1}, Y_0 and Y_1. Therefore, while making comparison the data of year Y_{-2} has been treated as the data for the year Y_0.

15. PLAN OF STUDY

The entire study has been divided into 5 Chapters. The first part of **Chapter - I** is meant to deal with the takeover phenomenon in general and takeovers as a strategy of turnaround in particular. The discussion pertaining to the objectives, hypotheses and methodology of the study is made in the second part of Chapter - I. An attempt has been made to study the liquidity of the sample units and its changes over the post-takeover period in **Chapter - II. Chapter - III** is intended to study the leverage of the sample units over the study period and the consequences of these changes on solvency, liquidity and profitability of the firms. The first part of **Chapter - IV** analyses the profitability of the sample units. Further, a comparison is made, in this chapter, with a particular reference to the profit position prevailing in the firms before and after the takeover periods. The second part of this chapter attempts to verify whether the better - known Management are able to turnaround the units faster and whether the firms are expanding after the takeover. **Chapter - V**, the final chapter, presents a summary of the study, conclusions arrived at in the respective chapters and offers a few suggestions for implementation by the units and authorities concerned.

REFERENCES

1. Golbe, Devsa L., and White, Lawrence J., *A Time - Series Analysis of Mergers and Acquisitions in the U.S. Economy*, Chapter 9 in Alan J. Auerbach, ed., (1988), *Corporate Takeovers: Causes and Consequences*, The University of Chicago Press, Chicago, pp. 265-309.
2. Weston, Fred J., Chung, Kwang S., and Hoag, Susan E. (1996), *Mergers, Restructuring and Corporate Control*, Prentice-Hall of India Pvt. Ltd., New Delhi.
3. Steiner, Peter O. (1977), *Mergers: Motives, Effects, Policies*, University of Michigan Press, Ann Arbor.
4. Goble, Devsa L., and White, Lawrence J., (1988), *op. cit.*
5. Weston, Fred J., Chung, Kwang S., and Hoag, Susan E. (1996), *op. cit.*
6. Markham, Jesse U. (1955), *Survey of Evidence and Findings on Mergers, Business Concentration and Price Policy*, Princeton University Press, Princeton, N.J., p. 156.
7. Stingler, George J. (1950), "Monopoly and Oligopoly by Merger," *American Economic Review*, May, 50, pp. 68-96.
8. Markhan, J.L. (1955), *op. cit.*
9. Stocking, G.W. (1955), *Commentary on Markham, Survey of Guidance and Findings on Mergers, in Business Concentration and Price Policy*, Princeton University Press, Princeton, N.J. pp. 191-211.
10. Stingler, George J. (1951), "The Division of Labor is Limited by the Extent of the Market," *Journal of Political Economy*, June 1951, pp. 185-193.
11. Butters, J.K., John Lintner, and W.L. Cary (1951), *Effect of Taxation on Corporate Mergers*, Harvard University Press, Cambridge, M.A.
12. Cooke, Terence E. (1986), *Mergers and Acquisitions*, Basil Blackwell Ltd., Oxford.
13. Grene, Thomas L. (1897), *Corporation Finance*, Pitman, New York.
14. Mead, Edwards, (1910), *Corporation Finance*, Appleton, New York.
15. Dewing, Arther Stone (1914), *Corporate Promotions and Reorganisation*, Harvard University Press, Cambridge.

16. Markham (1955), *Op. cit.*

17. Stocking (1955), *Op. cit.*

18. Stingler (1950), *Op. cit.*

19. Butters, J.K., John Lintner, and W.L. Cary (1951), *Op. cit.*

20. Kelly, E.M. (1967), *The Profitability of Growth through Merger*, Pennsylvania State University, State University.

21. Reid, Samuel R. (1968), *Mergers, Managers and the Economy*, McGraw-Hill, New York.

22. Kelly (1967), *Op. cit.*

23. Hagarty, Thomas P. (1970), "The Profitability of Corporate Mergers," *Journal of Business*, 43 (3) July, 70, pp. 317-327.

24. Franks, et al. (1976), *An Industry Study of the Profitability of Mergers*, London School of Business Studies, Institute of Finance and Accounting Discussion Paper.

25. Gort, Michael (1962), *Diversification and Integration in American Industry*, Princeton University Press, Princeton.

26. Halpern, P.J. (1973), "Empirical Estimates of the Amount and Distribution of Gaints to Companies in Mergers," *Journal of Business*, 46, pp. 554-575.

27. Gagon, J.M., et al. (1982), "Stock Market Behaviour of Merging Firms," *European Economic Review*, 17, pp. 187-211.

28. Weston, J. Fred. and Mansighka, Surendra K. (1971), "Tests of the Efficiency Performances of conglomerate Firms," *Journal of Finances*, 26 (4) Sept 71, pp. 919-946.

29. Lev. Baruch, and Mandelkar, Gershon, (1972), "The Micro Economic Consequences of Mergers," *Journal of Business*, 45 (1) Jan. 72, pp. 795-802.

30. Hayes Samuel L. III and Taussig, Russell A. (1967), "Tactics of Cash Takeover Bids," *Harvard Business Review*, 45 (2) March – April, 67, pp. 135.

31. Singh, Ajit (1971), *Takeovers: Their Relevance to the Stock Market and Theory of the Firm*, Cambridge University Press, Cambridge.

32. Boyle, Stanley (1970), "Pre-Merger Growth and Profit United States 1948-1968," *St. John's Law Review*, Special Edition, Spring, 70, pp. 152-170.

33. FTC Report (1970), *Current Trends in Merger Activity*, Report No. 8, United States Government Printing Office, Washington, D.C.

34. Binder, Denis (1973), "Securities Law of Contested Tender Offers," *New York Law Forum*, 16 (3) Winter, 73, pp. 569-679.

35. Hindley, Brain, (1970), "Separation of Ownership and Control in the Modern Corporation," *Journal of Law and Economics*, 13 (1), pp. 185-221.

36. Kelly (1967), *Op. cit.*

37. Reid, Samuel (1968), *Op. cit.*

38. Hogarty (1970), *Op. cit.*

39. Gort, Thomas F. (1970), "New Evidence on Mergers," *Journal of Law and Economics* 13 (16), pp. 167-184.

40. Lev, Baruch, and Gershon Mandlker (1972), *Op. cit.*

41. Kaveri, V.S. (1986), *Financial Analysis of Company Mergers in India*, Himalaya Publishing House.

42. Roy, Malay, K. (1986), *Takeover: A Corporate Finance Approach*, Unpublished ICSSR Project Study.

43. Ashok Kumar, N., and Parchure, Rajas (1990), *Mergers and Takeovers in India*, The Times Research Foundations, Pune.

Chapter II

LIQUIDITY ANALYSIS

The purpose of this chapter is to outline the principles of liquidity management, to measure the liquidity in selected sample companies before and after the takeover and, to identify whether there is any improvement in the liquidity position of the sample companies after the takeover.

1. HYPOTHESIS

In order to achieve the above objectives, the following Hypothesis has been set:

When a takeover of a sick company occurs, the company should turnaround and achieve better liquidity, particularly the short-term liquidity.

2. CONCEPT OF LIQUIDITY

The term 'liquidity' means the debt-repaying capacity of an undertaking. It refers to the firm's ability to meet the claims of suppliers of goods and services, and creditors. According to Archer and D' Ambrosio, liquidity means cash and cash availability, and it is from current operations and previous accumulations that cash is available, to take care of the claims of both the short-term suppliers of capital and the long-term ones.[1] It has two dimensions; the short term and the long-term liquidity.

Short-term liquidity implies the capacity of the

undertaking, repay the short-term debt, which means the same as the ability of the firm in meeting the currently maturing obligations from out of the current assets. The purpose of the short-term analysis is to derive a picture of the firm to meet its short-term obligations out of its short-term resources that is, to estimate the risk of supplying short-term capital to the firm.

Analysis of the firm's long-term liquidity position refers to the ability of the firm to meet its long-term financial obligations such as interest and dividend payment and repayment of principal. Long-term liquidity refers to the ability of the firm to retire long-term debt and interest and other long-run obligations. When relationships are established along these lines, it is assumed that in the long-run assets could be liquidated to meet the financial claims of the firm. Quite often, the expression 'liquidity' is used to mean short-term liquidity of the companies.[2] It is in this sense working capital is viewed as a 'liquidation concept'.

In this chapter it is proposed to study the liquidity of the firms in short-term context, that is their ability to pay-off current liabilities. Liquidity from long-term angle is studied in another chapter entitled **"Leverage Analysis.**

3. IMPORTANCE OF LIQUIDITY

Any company, no matter how big or small, moves on cash and not on profits. You can't pay bills with profits, only cash. You can't pay employees with profits, only cash. Everybody wants to know whether you have got any cash. unfortunately, many companies that make big profits, suffer by want of money. It does not matter whether your industry is high tech or low tech. In the end, you need to have enough money to pay your obligations or you will go out of business.[3]

One may be wondering why liquidity is a matter of such a serious concern. Since, the firm possesses short-term liabilities, which it has to meet at face value when they are due, it should have sufficient money to meet those demands. If a firm cannot meet these liabilities, its existence is threatened and, along with it, the future streams of returns to shareholders. Thus, liquidity threatens the shareholder's wealth.

Liquidity of a business is one of the key factors that determine its propensity for success or failure. Both excess and shortage of liquidity affects the interests of the firm. By excess liquidity in a firm, it is meant that it is carrying higher current assets than are warranted by the requirements of production. Hence, it indicates the blocking up of funds in current assets without any return. Besides, the firm has to incur costs to carry them overtime. Further, the value of such assets would depreciate in times of Inflation, if they were left idle. Owing to cornering of capital, the firm may have to resort to additional borrowing even at a fancy rates on the other hand, the impact of inadequate liquidity is more severe. Production may have to be curtailed or stopped for want of necessary funds. If the firm is not in a position to pay off the debts, the credit-worthiness of the firm is badly affected. The smaller the amount of default, the higher would be the damage done to the image of any firm. In addition, the firm will not be able to secure funds from outside sources, and the existing creditors may even force the firm into bankruptcy.[4] Further, insufficient funds will not allow the firm to launch any profitable project or earn attractive rates of return on the existing investment.

Between the excess and inadequate liquidity, the latter is considered to be more detrimental, since the lack of liquidity may endanger the very existence of the business enterprise. Besides, both the excess and inadequate liquidity adversely affect the profitability, whereas liquidity *per se* is influenced by the low profitability.

4. MEASUREMENTS OF LIQUIDITY

K.V. Rao,[5] suggests that the liquidity of an enterprise can be studied in two ways, namely, (1) Technical liquidity and (2) Operational liquidity. The difference between the two methods of liquidity measurement depends upon whether one assumes the 'liquidation concept' of business as in case of the Technical liquidity or the 'going concern concept' of business as in the case of the operational liquidity.

The first method of computation of liquidity is based on the assumption that the firm might become insolvent at any time and whether, in such an event, the current assets held by the undertaking would be sufficient to pay-off the current liabilities. On the other hand, the computation of operational liquidity attempts the measurement of the firm's potential to meet the current obligations on the basis of net cash flows originating from out of its own operations.[6] It is assumed under this approach, that firms are going firms and hence the liabilities are met through the net cash flows arising out of their operations.[7]

4.1. Technical Liquidity

Technical liquidity is normally evaluated on the basis of current ratio, Acid Test (Quick) ratio and Absolute liquidity ratio. These ratios are calculated on the basis of balance sheet information of a company and these have been the most traditional measures of company liquidity.

a. Current Ratio: This ratio expresses the relation between current assets and current liabilities. It is calculated by dividing current assets with current liabilities.

$$\text{Current Ratio} = \frac{\text{Current Assets}}{\text{Current Liabilities}}$$

It indicates the availability of current assets in rupees for every one rupee of current liabilities. A high ratio means that the firm has more investment in current assets. While a low ratio indicates that the firm in question is unable to retire its current liabilities. In fact, a satisfactory current ratio for any given firm is difficult to judge.

b. Quick or Acid Test Ratio: Recognising that inventory might not be very liquid or slow moving, this ratio takes the quickly realisable assets and measures them against current liabilities. This is a more refined, if somewhat conservative, estimate of the firm's liquidity, since it established a relation between quick or liquid assets and current liabilities. To be precise, a quick asset is one that can be converted into cash immediately or reasonably soon without loss of value. Inventory and period expenses are considered to be less liquid. Inventories normally require some time for realising into cash. The quick ratio is then, expressed as a relation between quick assets and current liabilities, as

$$\text{Quick Ratio} = \frac{\text{Quick Assets}}{\text{Current Liabilities}} = \frac{\text{Current Assets - Inventories}}{\text{Current Liabilities}}$$

This ratio does not entirely supplant the current ratio, rather, it partially supplements current ratio and when used in conjunction with it, tends to give a better picture of the firm's ability to meet its claims out of short-term assets.

c. **Absolute Liquidity Ratio:** This ratio is the refinement of the concept of eliminating inventory as liquid asset in the acid-test ratio, because of their uncertain value at the time of liquidation. Although, receivables are generally much more liquid in nature than inventories, some doubt may exist concerning their liquidity as well. So, by eliminating receivables and inventories from the current assets, another measure of liquidity is derived by relating the sum of cash and marketable securities to the current liabilities. This ratio can be expressed as

$$\text{Absolute Liquid ratio} = \frac{\text{Cash + marketable securities}}{\text{Current liabilities}}$$

or

$$= \frac{\text{Current Assets - Inventory - Receivables}}{\text{Current liabilities}}$$

All the above three ratios are essentially static and present only a snapshot view of the things. Quite often these fail to capture the dynamic nature of company's liquidity.

4.2. Operational Liquidity: Operational liquidity which is based on the going concern concept of a business, is determined by expressing cash flows as a percentage of current liabilities.

Early sixties witnessed the development of two new measures of business liquidity, viz., the Bierman's measure[8] and the Benston and Sorter's measure.[9] Though these measures attempted to relate a flow variable to a stock, the exercise on the whole remained static and snapshot.[10]

Lemke[11]proposed a different set of indices for evaluating company liquidity, which seemingly offered a major advance over the existing measures as he clearly recognised the primacy of cash flow data in judging the liquidity of a business. However, the operationalisation of Lemke's indices assumed the availability of detailed cash flow data, often inaccessible to those outside the company.

In the light of this, S.P. Parashar,[12] suggested a framework for measuring a company liquidity. He has envisaged the following four basic indices and three summary indices for measuring liquidity.

The basic indices

1. The priority cash outflow Index

$$= \frac{\text{Total priority cash out flow}}{\text{Total operating assets}} \times 100$$

2. Discretionary cash outflow Index

$$= \frac{\text{Total discretionary cash outflow}}{\text{Total operating assets}} \times 100$$

3. Operational cash inflow Index

$$= \frac{\text{Total Operational cash inflow}}{\text{Total operating assets}} \times 100$$

4. Financial cash inflow index

$$= \frac{\text{Total financial cash inflow}}{\text{Total operating assets}} \times 100$$

Summary Indices

5. Operational Liquidity Index = (3-1)
6. Financial Liquidity Index = (4-2)
7. Company's Liquidity Index = (5+6)

The rationale behind the construction of these indices is that the priority cash outflow index and operational cash inflow index will indicate the variations in the routine cash outflows and cash inflows, respectively. The discretionary cash outflow and financial cash inflow index, on the other hand, indicate the variations in the not-so-routine cash outflows and cash inflows respectively. A trend analysis of these individual indices may be useful for understanding the direction of movement of liquidity of a company that is, whether it is improving or deteriorating, and also the reasons for that.

The three summary indices would be useful in monitoring the liquidity of a company on an aggregative and a disaggregate basis. The operational liquidity index would indicate the liquidity of a company in terms of its routine cash inflows and outflows. The financial liquidity index would, on the other hand, indicate the liquidity of a company in terms of its not-so-routine cash inflows and outflows, the company's liquidity index would indicate the overall liquidity of a company in aggregate terms. Thus the set of four basic and three summary indices may be expected to facilitate appraising the liquidity of a business firm in sufficient depth and detail.

ANALYSIS OF LIQUIDITY

In the light of the above discussion the analysis has been done in the framework given below:

1. Technical Liquidity Analysis
2. Net Working Capital Analysis
3. Operational Liquidity Analysis
4. Percentages Analysis
5. Decomposition Analysis
6. Analysis of sources and uses and Diversion of funds

Now, Let us first discuss the technical liquidity, net working capital and operational liquidity for the sample cases.

5. ANALYSIS OF TECHNICAL LIQUIDITY

As stated earlier, there are three ratios to verify this liquidity. They are: (1) Current ratio, (2) Quick ratio and (3) Absolute liquidity ratio.

5.1. Current Ratio: Current Ratio is a measure of firm's short-term solvency. In other words this ratio tells the ability of the firm to meet its short-term obligations. This ratio indicates the proportion of current assets available for current liabilities. The larger the amount of current assets available for current liabilities, the more the firm's ability to meet the current obligations and the greater the safety of funds of short-term creditors.

Though, there is no hard and fast rule conventionally, a current ratio of 2:1 is considered satisfactory. This means that for every one rupee of current liabilities, there needs to be two rupees worth of current assets. This is said to be a satisfactory situation. The logic behind this conventional rule is that even if there is a drop of 50 per cent in the value of the current assets, a firm can still meet its hundred per cent obligations without

Table - 2.1: Current Ratio of the Sample Units

(Times)

Years / *Companies*	Y_{-4}	Y_{-3}	Y_{-2}	Y_{-1}	Y_{0}	Y_{1}	Y_{2}	Y_{3}	Y_{4}	Y_{5}	Y_{6}
Dempo Dairy	0.48	0.52	0.41	0.49	0.70	1.41	1.72	2.53	NA	x	x
ICML	NA	NA	NA	NA	0.22	1.60	1.71	2.04	2.29	x	x.
Amar Dye-Chem	0.94	1.07	1.11	0.66	0.89	0.64	0.48	x	x	x	x
Bokiyu Tanneries	0.28	0.20	0.22	0.23	0.34	0.64	0.75	1.16	1.24	1.11	x.
India Precision	0.40	0.46	0.39	0.32	0.98	1.68	0.99	0.79	0.80	3.41	2.33
Coromandal Pharma	NA	NA	NA	0.07	0.08	2.53	1.15	1.71	1.08	x	x.
Mico Farm Chem	NA	NA	NA	0.09	3.30	2.59	2.03	2.00	1.46	1.44	x
Sivamani Spinning	0.53	0.19	0.19	NA	NA	NA	0.32	0.44	0.77	NA	x

Note: 'NA' Indicates data not available , and 'x' indicates the years beyond the year Y_n

Source: Annual Reports and other published information of various companies. Since, the source is the same for the entire table this is not being repeated for each of the table.

any problem from the remaining 50 per cent of the current assets. However, this rule of thumb can not be applied mechanically. The satisfactory current ratio would depend on various factors like the capital market position, the availability of long-term as well as short-term funds to finance current assets, the nature of the Industry and so on.

Though, normally a firm with higher current ratio has better liquidity, a very high current ratio may also sometimes be treated as not a healthy trend. "It is important to note that a very high ratio of current assets to current liabilities may be indicative of slack management practices, as it might signal excessive inventories for the current requirements and poor credit management in terms of over-extended accounts receivables. At the same time, the firm may not be making full use of its current borrowing capacity".[13] Therefore, a firm should have neither a very high nor a low current ratio, but a reasonable ratio.

If one studies the information presented in table - 2.1 carefully, one can find some companies with steadily increasing ratios and some more companies, though have a better ratio after takeover, do not follow any particular trend and yet some more have a declining ratio. Let us now study the details.

The following companies have an increasing trend in current ratio:

1. Dempo Dairy
2. ICML
3. Bokiyu Tanneries
4. Sivamani Spinning

Bokiyu Tanneries had a continuously increasing current ratio till year Y_4 and there had been a slight decline of current ratio from 1.24:1 to 1.11:1 in the year Y_5. The reason for this is that there has been a more increase in current liabilities than increase in current assets in the year Y_5. Consequently, the ratio has come down. Sivamani spinning also though had an increasing current ratio it had been very much below 1:1.

Some other companies though have a better ratio, there were frequent increases and decreases in it even after the takeover. They are -

2. India Precision, and
3. Coromandal Pharma

There are two companies, which have declining current ratios after the takeover period. They are:

1. Amar Dye-Chem, and
2. Mico Farm Chemicals

Mico Farm Chemicals though had a declining trend, its current ratios are reasonably better, ranging from 3.30:1 in the year Y_0 to 1.44:1 in the year Y_5. May be the company had followed this declining trend deliberately to reduce the excessive current asset and bring them to reasonable levels.

Amar Dye-Chem has a peculiar trend with better current ratios before the takeover and after the takeover it is gradually declining. It had been continuously declining after the takeover and reached a level of 0.48:1 which is a sign of illiquidity.

If we analyse the times the current assets are covering current liabilities, the following picture emerges:

Dempo Dairy had started from 0.48:1 times in year Y_{-4} and gradually increased to 2.53:1 by the year Y_3. This is a sound ratio as it is higher than the generally accepted norm of 2:1. ICML had started with a ratio of 0.32:1 in the year Y_0 and increased to 2.29:1 in the year Y_4. It is a good ratio and the company should try to maintain at that level without any further major increases or decreases, as these would effect either profitability or liquidity of the company.

Amar Dye-Chem started the ratio with 0.89:1 in year Y_0 and has reached to 0.48:1 by the year Y_2. There was almost a continuous decline in the ratio with an exception of one or two years. This is not a healthy sign.

Bokiyu Tanneries, though showed a sign of continuous improvement till the year Y_4 with 1.24:1, it had declined in the year Y_5. It has a ratio of 1.11:1 in year Y_5. The company should maintain this ratio at least at the level of year Y_1 (i.e 1.84:1) or slightly at a higher level.

India precision had a good ratio in the year Y_1 at 1.68:1, but subsequently it had kept on declining to reach 0.80:1 by the year Y_4. The current ratio had increased steeply to 3.41:1 by the year Y_5 and again declined to 2.33:1 by the year Y_6. This steep increase in the ratio in the year Y_5 was due to an increase in the current assets and a sharp decline in the current liabilities. Since, this ratio was too high in the next year, probably, it was brought down to acceptable level by increasing current liabilities and by slightly decreasing the current assets.

Coromandal Pharma also recovered its ratio after the takeover. It had been maintaining a ratio of more than 1:1 after the takeover. In the year Y_1 the ratio was 2.53:1 when compared to 0.08:1 in the year Y_o. However, it had dropped down to 1.15:1 in the year Y_3 and again increased to 1.71:1. There has been a very wide fluctuation in the current ratio of this company. The reason for this abnormal change in the year Y_1 from year Y_o was about six-fold increase in the current assets and a five-fold decrease in the current liabilities.

Mico Farm Chemicals has a very high ratio in the year y_o at 3.30:1. Subsequently, the company had reduced this ratio and came down to the levels of 2:1 by the year Y_3. However the declining trend continued further and the current ratio had reached to 1.44:1 by the year Y_5. But this decline to below 2:1 was not normally a healthy sign and the company should reach the ratio of 2:1.

Sivamani spinning always had a current ratio of less than 1:1. However, the current ratio had been on a continuously increasing trend after the takeover. From the above discussion, it may be concluded that a majority of the sample companies have better current ratio in the post-takeover period. This is as a result of turnaround efforts made by the new managements.

5.2. Acid Test or Quick Ratio: Recognising that inventory might not be very liquid or slow-moving, this ratio takes the quickly realisable assets into account and measures them against current liabilities.

This ratio is a more refined and rigorous measure of a firm's ability to service short-term liabilities. The usefulness of the ratio lies in the fact that it is widely accepted as the best available test of the liquidity position of a firm. This ratio is a more rigorous and penetrating test of liquidity position of a firm. As a general rule, an acid test ratio of 1:1 is considered satisfactory. This is because the firm can meet its current claims easily, as the quick assets can be easily converted into cash without loss of much time and value.

As stated earlier this ratio does not completely supplant the current ratio, rather it partially supplements current ratio and when used in conjunction with it, tends to give a better picture of the firm's ability to meet its claims out of the short-term assets.

In the present analysis, Table - 2.2 presents a picture of the Quick Ratios of all the sample companies at a glance. If one carefully analyses Table - 2.2, one can classify the sample companies into three groups. They are:

1. Companies with increasing Quick ratio after the takeover like-
    1. Dempo Dairy
    2. ICML
    3. Bokiyu Tanneries
    4. Sivamani Spinning
2. Companies with mixed Quick ratios like:
    1. Coromandal Pharma
    2. India Precision, and
3. Companies with declining Quick ratio even in the post-takeover period like -
    1. Amar Dye-Chem
    2. Mico Farm Chemicals.

Table - 2.2: Quick Ratio of the Sample Units

(Times)

Companies / *Years*	Y_{-4}	Y_{-3}	Y_{-2}	Y_{-1}	Y_0	Y_1	Y_2	Y_3	Y_4	Y_5	Y_6
Dempo Dairy	0.14	0.20	0.15	0.12	0.06	0.96	1.32	1.72	NA	x	x
ICML	NA	NA	NA	NA	0.13	1.03	1.40	1.48	1.81	x	x
Amar Dye-Chem	0.48	0.55	0.58	0.34	0.45	0.33	0.26	x	x	x	x
Bokiyu Tanneries	0.13	0.13	0.10	0.10	0.16	0.22	0.34	0.67	1.04	0.83	x
India Precision	0.13	0.12	0.18	0.11	0.36	0.71	0.31	0.25	0.24	1.23	0.95
Coromandal Pharma	NA	NA	NA	0.07	0.08	1.74	0.59	1.20	1.01	x	x
Mico Farm Chem	NA	NA	NA	0.01	1.49	1.63	1.47	1.33	1.18	1.13	x
Sivamani Sping	0.28	0.11	0.12	NA	NA	NA	0.16	0.20	0.42	NA	x

Note: 'NA' indicates data not available, and 'X' indicates years beyond year Y_n

It may be mentioned that Bokiyu Tanneries had an ever increasing quick ratio till the year Y_4. However, in the year Y_5, there has been a decrease in the ratio to 0.83:1. The reason for this was the increase in the quick assets was less than the increase in the current liabilities.

An analysis of the levels of quick ratio of sample units, the following picture emerges:

Dempo Dairy had a fluctuating quick ratio before the takeover period and it had a very low ratio of 0.06:1. However, from the year Y_1 onwards it has been steadily increasing and reached to 1.72:1 in the year Y_3. This is on the higher side of the general levels and the company may try to reduce it to generally accepted levels depending upon its circumstances.

ICML also had a very low quick ratio in the year of takeover (Y_0) at 0.13:1. However, it had improved gradually from year y_1 and reached to 1.81:1 in the year Y_4. This company also may consider reducing its quick ratio in order to put the excess quick assets into profitable use.

Amar Dye-Chem never had a quick ratio of 1:1 in the entire period of study. Further, the quick ratio had been on a declining trend in the post takeover period.

As mentioned above Bokiyu Tanneries had continuously increasing quick ratio in the post-takeover period except in the year Y_5. Though, it had a ratio of 0.14:1 in the year Y_0, it reached to generally acceptable levels in the year Y_4 and slightly declined to 0.83:1 in the year Y_5.

India Precision Bearings had a ratio of 0.36:1 in the year Y_0 and increased to 0.71:1 by the year Y_1. Thereafter from the year Y_2 onwards it had a declining trend. However, the company had improved its quick ratio from the year Y_5 and brought this ratio back to acceptable levels and maintained it there, even in the year Y_6.

Coromandal Parma had better quick ratio in the post takeover, period, though changing from year to year.

Mico Farm Chemicals also had been maintaining higher

quick ratio in the post- takeover period. It had a ratio of about 1.5:1 till year Y_2. However, from year Y_3 onwards it had a declining quick ratio and reached to a level of 1.13:1, which is closer to the generally accepted average ratio of 1:1. The company should maintain this ratio around these levels.

Sivamani Spinning never had quick ratio of more than 0.50:1. There was an increasing trend immediately after the takeover.

To conclude, most of sample companies have good quick ratios in the post-takeover period.

5.3. Absolute liquidity ratio: Absolute liquidity ratio is a further refinement of the concept of eliminating inventory as liquid assets in the acid-test ratio. In this ratio, receivables are eliminated in addition to the inventory from the current assets and a comparision is made with current liabilities. This ratio is calculated by dividing the super-quick assets by the current liabilities of a firm.

Although receivables are generally much more liquid in nature than inventories, some doubt may exist concerning their liquidity as well. So, by eliminating receivables and inventories from the current assets, another measure of liquidity is derieved by relating the sum of cash and marketable securities to the current liabilities. Generally, an absolute liquidity ratio of 0.5:1 is considered appropriate in evaluating liquidity.[14].

In the present study, however, the super-quick assets (i.e. cash and marketable securities) are generally very negligible. Therefore, it has been decided not to calculate this ratio.

Though, one would evaluate liquidity on the basis of current and liquid ratios, there may be a situation where the evaluation becomes difficult. It is difficult particularly, when some companies have high current ratios but low quick ratios and other companies have low current ratios but high quick ratios. In such cases, it is difficult to state which of these companies are good and which are bad. Therefore, there is a need for a parameter, which includes both these two ratios in it.

6. NET WORKING CAPITAL

Working capital is used in different connotations by different writers. Obviously it is understood either as the total of current assets or as the excess of current assets over current liabilities. The former is referred to as the gross working capital and the latter as the net working capital. The net working capital describes that part of the current asset investment, financed from long-term capital financing sources. The remaining part of current assets financing is necessarily provided by the current liabilities.

In the present study Table -2.3, presents a picture of the Net Working Capital (NWC) position of the sample companies. The general yard stick for measuring liquidity here is that if the NWC is positive then the company is having a good liquidity and if it is negative, then the company is having a bad liquidity. Because it would not be in a position to meet its current liabilities through its current assets which is not a healthy situation for a company. It is evident from the information that four types of behavioural trends can be seen among the companies selected for this study. They are:

1. Companies having generally positive and increasing NWC in the post-takeover period, like -
   a. Dempo Dairy
   b. Mico Farm Chemicals
2. Companies having a mix of both positive and negative trends in NWC in the post-takeover period, like:
   a. ICML
   b. Bokiyu Tanneries
   c. Coromandal Pharma
   d. India Precision
3. Company with an increasing negative net working capital in the post-takeover period, like: Amar Dye-Chem

4. and, the company with a negative net working capital but showing a declining trend in the post-takeover period, like: Sivamani spinning

Let us now see how the individual companies performed with regard to net working capital over the years.

Dempo Dairy, though started with a negative net working capital has became positive by the year Y_1 and later on it has steadily improved.

ICML had a negative NWC in the year Y_0, but improved from the year Y_1 and has been positive henceforth. However, there has been a decline in the net working capital in the year Y_2, when compared to year Y_1. The reason for this is, there has been a decline in the current assets and current liabilities and decline in current liabilities is more than the decline in the current assets. In the years Y_3 and Y_4, there has been an increasing trend.

Amar Dye-Chem has a very interesting trend. It had good amounts of net working capital before the takeover and had negative net working capital from year Y_0 and the trend had been continuous and ever increasing, but negatively.

Bokiyu Tanneries had a negative NWC and it had been positive from the year Y_3 only. It has been steadily increasing in the post-takeover period, though there has been a decline in the year Y_5.

India Precision Bearings though had a positive net working capital in the year Y_1, it had been negative and continuously increasing till the year Y_4. The reason for the positive NWC in the year Y_1 was, a marginal increase in the current asset but a good decline in current liabilities. However, in the years Y_5 and Y_6, there had been huge amounts of net working capital. This had resulted from huge declines in current liabilities and significant increases in current assets.

Coromandal Pharma, had a negative NWC before the takeover but there has been a positive NWC in the post-takeover period. However, there had been frequent fluctuations from year to year.

Table - 2.3: Net Working Capital of the Sample Units

(Rs. in lakh)

Companies \ Years	Y_{-4}	Y_{-3}	Y_{-2}	Y_{-1}	Y_0	Y_1	Y_2	Y_3	Y_4	Y_5	Y_6
Dempo Dairy	-204.03	-215.70	-311.56	-150.32	-20.00	23.00	79.00	144.00	NA	x	x
ICML	NA	NA	NA	NA	-163.26	213.62	194.81	292.81	384.98	x	x
Amar Dye-Chem	-145.12	163.01	269.75	1030.09	-446.33	-1752.28	-2963.37	x	x	x	x
Bokiyu Tanneries	-113.06	-154.19	-169.31	-197.55	-135.53	-103.10	-80.29	64.93	263.06	187.14	x
India Precision	-201.00	30.61	7.06	-397.00	-7.65	137.93	-4.63	-127.94	-136.27	523.97	410.12
Coromandal Pha	NA	NA	NA	-100.25	-104.32	25.88	12.07	84.19	24.76	x	x
Mico Farm Chem	NA	NA	NA	-166.29	134.85	232.95	275.37	266.59	287.30	304.72	x
Sivamani Spining	-37.30	-49.85	-54.4	NA	NA	NA	-261.81	-209.08	-73.99	NA	x

Note: NA indicates data not available ,and, 'X' indicates years beyond year Y_n

Mico Farm Chemicals, had a negative NWC in the year Y_{-1} and subsequently, it had all positive values of NWC except in the year Y_3, where there was a slight decrease.

Sivamani spinning, also had a negative net working capital even in the post-takeover period, but with a declining trend.

On the whole, it can be concluded that the net working capital of most of the companies has been positive for most of the years.

7. NET CASHFLOWS AND OPERATIONAL LIQUIDITY

As stated earlier, the operational liquidity measures the firm's potential to meet its current obligations on the basis of net cash flows originating from its own operations.

This approach assumes that the units are going on firms and hence, the liabilities are to be met through the net cash flows arising out of their operations. As is evident from the data, there was no profit after tax, in the entire study period except for three years and in two companies. This is because of the reason that most of the companies were (are) sick and some have gradually reduced (reducing) their accumulated losses. Consequently, there are no provisions for taxation thereby no Profit After Tax (PAT). Therefore, the Profit Before Tax (PBT), has taken as PAT in this study while calculating the net cash flows. Now, let us examine how the net cash flows and operational liquidity had changed over the post-takeover years in each of the sample companies.

7.1. Net Cash flows

Table - 2.4 presents a picture of Net Cash flows over the years in all the sample companies. The net cash flows (NCF) were negative in the year of takeover (Y_0) in all the companies except in Amar Dye-Chem. However, subsequently, it had always been negative. The reason for this, was that there were reliefs and remissions included in the other income to the extent of Rs. 754.47 lakh, which had accrued in terms of the BIFR order in the year Y_0. If we deduct this amount from the net cash flows, there will be negative net cash flows. Hence strictly speaking, there were negative net cash flows to the tune of Rs. 60.64 lakh even in the year Y_0 in case of Amar Dye-Chem also.

Table - 2.4 : Net Cashflows of the Sample Units

(in Rs. lakhs)

Companies \ Years	Y_0	Y_1	Y_2	Y_3	Y_4	Y_5	Y_6
Dempo Dairy	–69.00	11.00	58.00	114.00	NA	x	x
ICML	-94.77	64.53	99.41	90.87	84.28	x	x
Amar Dye-Chem	693.83	-798.14	-811.00	x	x	x	x
Bokiyco Tanneries	-74.27	40.21	63.18	119.20	233.87	31.66	x
India Precision	-65.34	91.35	109.71	33.70	138.46	114.45	142.53
Coramandal Pharma	-54.75	-9.15	-35.91	-123.47	-188.35	x	x
Mico Farm Chemicals	-30.55	13.17	11.77	55.94	103.12	145.34	x
Sivamani Spg.	NA	NA	44.11	59.26	20.65	NA	x

Note: 'X' indicates years beyond Yn , 'NA' indicates data not available

On careful examination of trends in the table - 2.5, we can categorise the companies into three groups. They are:

1. Company with increasing net cash flows such as-
   a. Dempo Dairy
2. Companies with mixed trend with increases and decreases like -
   a. ICML
   b. Bokiyu Tanneries
   c. India precision
   d. Mico Farm Chemicals
   e. Sivamani Spinning, and
3. companies with negative net cash flows such as:
   a. Amar Dye-Chem
   b. Coromandal Pharma

Now, let us analyse cash flows over the years in each of the companies:

Dempo Dairy though had a negative net cash flow in the year Y_o, it had gradually improved over the years and reached to a level of Rs. 114.00 lakh by the year Y_3.

ICML had a negative NCF of Rs 94.77 lakh in the year Y_o and gradually improved to Rs. 99.41 lakh by the year Y_2 and started declining from the year Y_3 onwards. This declining trend is due to a decline in the PAT in the years Y_3 and Y_4.

Amar Dye-Chem had a negative NCF for the years Y_1 and Y_2 though it was positive in the year Y_o. As stated earlier the positive NCF in year Y_o was due to the inclusion of Rs. 754.47 lakh of reliefs and remissions in the other incomes of year Y_o.

Bokiyu Tanneries had a negative NCF in the year Y_o and became positive by the year Y_1 at Rs. 63.18 lakh and steadily increased to Rs. 233.87 lakh by the year Y_4 and finally dipped down to Rs. 31.66 lakh in the very next year (i.e. Y_5). This sudden dip in the NCF was due to huge amounts of gross loss and a steep increase in the interest burden. The company could manage a positive PBT only with the help of other incomes.

India Precision Bearings had generally an increasing trend in the NCF over the years except for the years Y_3 and Y_5. Like other companies, this also had a negative NCF in the year Y_o but had staged back with a positive NCF of Rs. 91.35 lakh by the year Y_1. The increase had continued even in the year Y_2, but it had dipped down to Rs. 33.70 lakh by the year Y_3. Again it had increased to Rs. 138.46 lakh in the year Y_4 but decreased to Rs. 114.45 lakh in the year Y_5, only to increase again in the year Y_6 to Rs. 142.53 lakh. The decline in net cash flows of this unit for the years Y_3 and Y_5 was mainly due to an increase in the cost of goods sold, which had reduced the PAT.

Coromandal Pharma always had a negative net cash flows from the year Y_o. However, in the year Y_1 the amount of negative net cash flows had reduced only to stage a continuous increase in the negative net cash flows till the latest year for which accounts are available (i.e. Y_4).

Mico Farm Chemicals also had a negative net cash flows in the year Y_o. Subsequently, it had all positive net cash flows in all the years of the post-takeover. The net cash flows had been continuously increasing except in the year Y_2 where it was Rs. 11.77 lakh which was marginally less. Thereafter, it had been continuously increasing to register an amount of 145.34 lakh in the year Y_5.

Sivamani Spinning had a positive net cash flow in the year Y_2 and increased to Rs. 59.26 lakh by the year Y_3 and reduced to almost 1/3 of the amount of year Y_3, in the year Y_4. In the year Y_4 it had a net cash flow of Rs. 20.65 lakh. This was mainly due to an increase in the cost of goods sold and the interest charges in the year Y_4.

To conclude, it may be noted that except the two sample units viz. Amar Dye-Chem and Coromandal Pharma, all other remaining units have positive NCF in the post takeover period.

7.2. Operational Liquidity

As pointed out earlier, what is more important for a firm is to retire the current liabilities from out of cash flows originating from their own operations. Thus, the concept of operational liquidity is a very useful measure of liquidity.

Table - 2.5 presents the relevant infromation in respect of the cash flows in percentage of current liabilities in the selected units for the study. If we analyse the trend of the operational liquidity of the sample firms, it is by and large following the similar trend as of net cash flows. If the proportion of net cash flows is hundred per cent or more to current liabilities, then there is good operational liquidity and if it is less, then the operational liquidity is not satisfactory. Now let us see how the operational liquidity has been changing in the sample firms over the post-takeover period. Whereever there negative NCF, we have not calculated operational liquidity ratio.

Table - 2.5: Operational Liquidity of the Sample Units

(in percentages)

Companies \ Years	Y_0	Y_1	Y_2	Y_3	Y_4	Y_5	Y_6
Dempo Dairy	+	19.64	52.73	121.28	NA	x	x
ICML	+	18.08	36.11	32.16	28.33	x	x
Amar Dye-Chem	17.5	+	+	x	x	x	x
Bokiyu Tanneries	+	14.17	19.31	29.82	21.69	1.87	x
India Precision	+	45.11	21.41	5.56	20.27	52.54	46.21
Coromandal Pharma	+	+	+	+	+	x	x
Mico Farm Chemicals	+	8.99	4.39	20.88	16.54	20.89	x
Sivamani Spinning	NA	NA	11.46	15.81	6.71	NA	x

Note: '+' indicates years with negative NCFs.
'x' indicates years beyond year Y_n.
'NA' indicates data not available.

Dempo Dairy had an operational liquidity ratio of 19.64 per cent in the year Y_1 and it had reached 121.28 per cent by the year Y_3. Of the entire sample units and over all the years of the study, this is the only company which had more than a hundred per cent of operating liquidity in the year Y_3. That is, the company had generated more net cash flows than the current liabilities.

ICML always had less than 40 per cent of operational liquidity ratio. Though, there is an increase in this ratio in the year Y_2 with 36.11 per cent from the year Y_1's 18.08 per cent, it had been gradually declining subsequently.

Amar Dye-Chem had positive NCF only in the year Y_0. Therefore, except in the year Y_0 the operational liquidity ratio has not been calculated.

Bokiyu Tanneries had an increasing operational liquidity ratio upto year Y_3 and there after it had been declining. It was as low as 1.87 per cent in the year Y_5. The reasons for this are gross loss and steep increase in the interest charges, as already stated.

India Precision Bearings had an operational liquidity ratio of 45.11 per cent in the year Y_1. Subsequently, it had a declining trend in the years Y_2 and Y_3 and again improved to 20.27 per cent in the year Y_4 and to 52.54 per cent in the year Y_5. Finally, the ratio was 46.21 per cent in the year Y_6.

Coromandal Pharma had negative net cash flows in all the years and thereby no operational liquidity ratio has been calculated.

Mico Farm Chemicals had a mixed operational liquidity ratios. There had been about 20 per cent ratio in the years Y_3 and Y_5, but a ratio of about 16 per cent in the year Y_4. This has happend inspite of an increase in the net cash flows of year Y_4. The reason for this was more than proportionate increase in the current liabilities.

Sivamani Spinning also had a mixed operational liquidity ratios. The ratio had never exceeded 15 per cent, except in the year Y_3, where it was marginally higher at 15.81 per cent.

To conclude it may be noted that, of the sample of eight units six units have positive operational liquidity ratios. They have improved their operational liquidity from negative value to as high as 121.28 per cent. This is a sign of turnaround of the takeover companies.

8. OTHER INDICES

In addition to current ratio, quick ratio and Net working capital, there are some proportions, which tells us the liquidity position of a company. They are:

1. Percentage of Quick Assets to Current Assets.
2. Percentage of Current Assets to Total Assets.
3. Percentage of Quick Assets to Total Assets.
4. Percentage of Current Liabilities to Total Debt.

The above 4 percentages tell us the proportions of various components of liquidity in relation to other assets and liabilities. Now let us examine, how these proportions are present in the sample companies and how they are changing over the period of time after the takeover.

8.1. Percentage of Quick Assets to Current Assets

This ratio/proportion would tell us, what percentage of Quick Assets are present in the Current Assets. This proportion tells that what proportion of the Current Assets can be easily converted into cash with in a short span of time. The difference in proportion of Current Assets and Quick Assets is the proportion of inventory to Current Assets. For example, if the Quick Assets are present to the level of 60 per cent in a company in its Current Assets, the remaining 40 per cent is the proportion of inventory to the current assets. Therefore, an increase in the proportion of quick assets in current assets of a firm implies that the firm has better liquidity. Table – 2.6 shows the proportion of quick assets to current assets company-wise over the study period.

Dempo Dairy has more than 60 per cent of Current Assets in the form of quick assets. In fact, it has been around 70 per cent from year Y_1 onwards. Within the quick assets, receivables occupied about 50 per cent of the total Current assets. Cash and Bank Balances also were in significant proportions in the post takeover period at about 20 per cent.

This ratio has been highest in the year Y_2 at 76.72 per cent. This was mainly due to an increase in the proportion of Cash and Bank Balances to 29.10 per cent.ICML also has more than 60 per cent of quick assets in its current assets. This proportion has been steadily increasing in the post-takeover period. The proportion has started with 59.36 per cent in the year Y_0 and it was at 78.94 per cent in the year Y_4. Sundry debtors and loans and advances occupied major proportions, even within the quick assets. Though, Cash and Bank Balances were initially in minor proportions, they have increased to more than 20 per cent in the years Y_3 and Y_4. There has been a mixed trend in the sundry debtors and loans and advances and generally, an increasing trend in the Cash and Bank balances.

Table - 2.6: Quick Assets as a Percentage of Current Assets for the Sample Units

(in percentages)

Companies \ Years	Y_0	Y_1	Y_2	Y_3	Y_4	Y_5	Y_6
Dempo Dairy	60.87	68.36	76.72	68.07	NA	x	x
ICML	59.36	64.14	64.82	72.44	78.94	x	x
Amar Dye-Chem	51.07	51.69	55.52	x	x	x	x
Bokiyu Tanneries	42.28	34.67	45.70	57.91	83.23	74.95	x
India Precision	37.31	42.34	31.69	31.73	30.18	36.14	40.93
Coromandal Pharma	97.53	68.96	51.40	69.96	92.73	x	x
Mico Farm Chemicals	45.15	62.94	72.27	66.70	81.03	78.64	x
Sivamani Spinning	61.65*	NA	49.01	44.46	54.65	NA	x

Notes: 'NA' indicates data not available.
'X' indicates years beyond year Y_n.
'*' Since data for year Y_0 was not available in case of Sivamani Spinning, the data of year Y_{-2} has been treated as Y_0.

Amar Dye-Chem had a steady proportion with more than 50 per cent of quick assets, present in current assets. Among the quick assets, sundry debtors, and loans and advances have occupied significant proportions. The proportion of sundry debtors was at about 40 per cent Cash and Bank balances have not been very significant.

Bokiyu Tanneries had a ratio of generally more than 40 per cent except in the year Y_1 where it was at 34.67 per cent Further, this proportion has been steadily increasing from year Y_1 to Y_4 and decreased by about 9 per cent in the year Y_5. Among the quick assets, sundry debtors occupied very major proportions followed by loans and advances. Cash and Bank balances and other current assets were in nominal proportions. The reason for a decrease in the proportion of quick assets in the year Y_5 was a decline in the proportions of sundry debtors and loans and advances.

The proportion of Quick Assets in the Current Assets had been fluctuating, in case of India Precision Bearings mostly between 30 per cent to 40 per cent. Except for the years Y_2, Y_3, and Y_4, this proportion had been more than 35 per cent for the remaining years, which means that there had been high proportion of inventory in the years Y_2, Y_3 and Y_4. This implies that during these years the firm had relatively less liquidity. However, in the years Y_5 and Y_6, the proportion had inproved to more than 35 per cent.

Coromandal Pharma had a very widely fluctauting proportion of quick assets to current assets. It was as high as 97.53 per cent in the year Y_0 and 92.73 per cent in the year Y_4. In the years Y_1 and Y_3, it was about 70 per cent and in the year Y_2 it was lowest at 51.40 per cent. Even within quick asset components, there has been wide changes from year to year, thus without following any steady trend.

Even in Mico Farm Chemicals, there had been regular changes in the proportions of quick assets to current assets from year to year. However, it has always been more than 60 per cent from year Y_1. The maximum proportion was highest in the year Y_4 at 81.03 per cent and minimum at 62.94 per cent in the year Y_1. The mixed trend can be seen even in quick assets components over years. A major proportion of quick assets has been occupied by sundry debtors. The highest proportion of sundry debtors to current assets was in the year Y_4 at 72.16 per cent. As a result of this even the proportion of quick assets to current assets was highest in the year Y_4.

Sivamani Spinning had quick assets to current assets proportion of 61.65 per cent in the year Y_{-2}. However, it had come down to 44.46 per cent by the year Y_3 and again increased to 54.65 per cent by the year Y_4. This implies that this unit has more than 50 per cent of current assets in the form of inventory for the years Y_2 and Y_3.

From the above discussion it may be concluded that most of the sample units have more than 50 per cent of the current assets in the form of quick assets and this proportion is on a generally increasing trend. This is a sign of better liquidity as a result of turnaround efforts by the new managements.

8.2. Percentage of Current Assets to Total Assets

This ratio tells us the proportion of current assets to total assets. This is an indicator of what was the proportion of current assets and fixed assets in the total assets and how it has been changing from year to year in the post-takeover years. Table 2.7 presents, how this proportion is changing over the years in each of the companies.

Table - 2.7 : Current Assets as a Percentage of Total Assets for the Sample Units

(in percentages)

Companies \ Years	Y_0	Y_1	Y_2	Y_3	Y_4	Y_5	Y_6
Dempo Dairy	17.10	28.52	51.50	60.25	NA	x	x
ICML	39.31	88.74	87.66	89.72	90.92	x	x
Amar Dye-Chem	69.96	71.33	69.09	x	x	x	x
Bokiyu Tanneries	77.13	79.26	32.47	50.66	76.19	83.12	x
India Precision	32.74	30.10	36.01	34.19	38.19	46.07	45.44
Coromandal Pharma	8.30	10.50	21.23	43.16	36.17	x	x
Mico Farm Chemicals	62.67	75.48	57.10	51.35	85.83	83.60	x
Sivamani Spinning	5.36*	NA	32.46	44.77	57.44	NA	x

Notes: 'NA' indicates data not available
'X' indicates years beyond year Y_n.
'*' indicates the data of year Y_{-2} has been treated as Y_0.

Dempo Dairy had an increasing current assets proportion in the total assets. It started with 17.10 per cent in the year Y_0 and had increased to 60.25 per cent by the year Y_3.

ICML has about 90 per cent of the total assets in the form of current assets after the takeover from the year Y_1. This means that the importance of working capital management is very high. Any small mismanagement in the working capital may lead to great losses and may up set the profitability.

Even the Amar Dye-Chem also had about 70 per cent of

total assets in the form of current assets. In this case also the importance of working capital is more.

Bokiyu Tanneries also has a current assets to total assets proportion of 75 per cent to 80 per cent in all the years except in the years Y_2 and Y_3 where it was 32.47 per cent and 50.66 per cent respectively. The reason for this lesser proportions in year Y_2 and Y_3 was disproportionate increases in the current assets and total assets. The increase in total assets was 233.74 per cent in the year Y_2 whereas the increase in current assets was 36.75 per cent. Similarly the increase in the total assets was 20.60 per cent and the increase in the current assets was 88.13 per cent in the year Y_3. Therefore, these disproportionate changes brought the proportion of current assets to total assets down in the years Y_2 and Y_3.

India precision had been having a stable proportion of current assets to total assets between 30 per cent to 40 per cent till the year Y_4. However, there were increases and decreases in this proportion and thereby showing a mixed trend. But in the years Y_5 and Y_6, the current assets proportion had increased in the total assets to about 45 per cent.

Coromandal Pharma had a steadily increasing proportion of current assets to total assets. It had a proportion of 8.30 per cent current assets to total assets in the year Y_0 and this proportion had increased upto 43.16 per cent by the year Y_3.

Mico Farm Chemicals though had a mixed trend with frequent increases and decreases even after the takeover period, it had always been more than 50 per cent. This proportion was minimum at 51.35 per cent in the year Y_3 and maximum at 85.83 per cent in the year Y_4. There has been a tremendous increase of about 35 per cent from year Y_3 to Y_4 in this proportion. This is because of the sudden increase of 52.70 per cent and 70.37 per cent in total assets and current assets respectively in the year Y_4.

In the case of Sivamani spinning the current assets were very low at 5.36 per cent in the year Y_0. However, it had gradually increased to 57.44 per cent by the year Y_4.

It may be concluded that six out of the eight sample units have more than 50 per cent of their assets in the form of current assets and their proportion has been gradually increasing.

8.3. Percentage of Quick Assets to Total Assets

This ratio tells us the proportion of quick assets to total assets. In other words this ratio reveals the presence of most liquid assets in the total assets and how the proportion was changing. Table – 2.8 shows, how this proportion has changed over years in each of the companies selected for sample.

Table - 2.8: Quick Assets as a Percentage of total Assets for the Sample Units

(In percentages)

Companies \ *Years*	Y_0	Y_1	Y_2	Y_3	Y_4	Y_5	Y_6
Dempo Dairy	10.27	19.50	39.51	41.01	NA	x	x
ICML	23.34	56.92	56.82	64.99	71.77	x	x
Amar Dye-Chem	35.73	36.87	38.36	x	x	x	x
Bokiyu Tanneries	32.61	27.48	14.84	29.34	63.41	62.30	x
India Precision	12.22	12.74	11.41	10.85	11.52	16.65	18.60
Coromandal Pharma	8.10	7.24	10.91	30.19	33.54	x	x
Mico Farm Chemicals	28.30	47.51	41.26	34.25	69.55	65.74	x
Sivamani Spinning	3.30	NA	22.41	25.62	39.25	NA	x

Note: 'NA' indicates data not available.
'X' indicates years beyond year Y_n.

As is evident from the information contained in the Table - 2.8, Dempo Dairy had a steady and regularly increasing presence of quick assets in the total assets. It started with a low of 10.27 per cent in the year Y_0 and reached to 41.01 per cent by the end of year Y_3.

ICML also had an ever-increasing and steady proportion of quick assets in total assets. This proportion was 23.34 per cent in the year Y_0 and reached to a maximum of 71.77 per cent by the year Y_4. This high proportion is also not in the interest of the company since high level of quick assets only leads to low turnover and low efficiency.

Amar Dye-Chem had a more stable and gradually increasing proportion of quick assets to total assets. The percentage had been always between 35 and 40. Bokiyu Tanneries had a mixed trend with wild fluctuations in the proportion of quick assets to current assets.

India Precision Bearings had a very stable proportion of quick assets to total assets. It had always fluctuated within a narrow range of 10 per cent to 14 per cent till year Y_4 and suddenly increased to 16.65 per cent and 18.60 per cent in the years Y_5 and Y_6 respectively.

Coromandal Pharma had an increasing trend in the proportion of quick assets to total assets. It started with 7.24 per cent in the year Y_1 and jumped to 30.19 per cent by the year Y_3 and closed at 33.54 per cent by the year Y_4.

Mico Farm Chemicals also had a mixed trend with wide fluctuations. The minimum proportion was 28.30 per cent in the year Y_0 and the maximum was 69.55 per cent in the year Y_4. There was a sudden increase in the proportion of quick assets to total assets in the year Y_4 and the same level continued even in the year Y_5 also.

Sivamani Spinning had a very low ratio of 3.30 per cent to begin with and the same increased to 39.25 per cent by the year Y_4.

It appears from the above discussion that the proportion of quick assets in the total assets also has been on an increasing trend and it has been more than 30 per cent in many cases.

8.4. Percentage of Current Liabilities to Total Debt

So far, all the above three proportions have taken various components of assets and are compared within themselves. However, this ratio has taken liabilities components into account and compared current liabilities with total debt.

This composition would tell what proportion of the total debt is in the form of current liabilities. Naturally, the remaining portion is occupied by the long-term debt. Table - 2.9 presents this proportion of each company over the post-takeover years.

Table - 2.9: Current Liabilities as a Percentage of Total Debt for the Sample Units

(In percentages)

Years / *Companies*	Y_0	Y_1	Y_2	Y_3	Y_4	Y_5	Y_n
Dempo Dairy	59.67	6.60	17.68	16.85	NA	x	x
ICML	30.80	30.91	28.63	28.75	29.55	x	x
Amar Dye-Chem	80.01	88.64	96.38	x	x	x	x
Bokiyu Tanneries	44.35	49.15	30.40	35.23	62.13	75.34	x
India Precision	19.83	12.83	28.43	33.39	38.52	11.33	19.51
Coromandal Pharma	27.19	4.71	17.63	24.21	36.50	x	x
Mico Farm Chemicals	13.37	23.44	33.89	34.25	58.55	63.88	x
Sivamani Spinning	23.71	NA	74.57	76.95	74.58	NA	x

Note: 'NA' indicates data not available.
'X' indicates years beyond year Y_n.

It can be seen from the Table - 2.9 that Dempo Dairy, though, had about 60 per cent of the current liabilities in the total debt in the year Y_0, reduced it to 6.60 per cent in the very next year (Y_1). However, from year Y_2 onwards it appears to be stabilised at about 15 per cent in the years Y_2 and Y_3.

ICML also had a balanced trend with very stable proportion of around 30 per cent. The minimum proportion was at 28.75 per cent in the year Y_3 and the maximum was at 30.91 per cent in the year Y_1.

Amar Dye-Chem, had a very high proportions of current liabilities to total debt in all the years with 80.01 per cent, 88.64 per cent and 96.38 per cent in the years Y_0, Y_1 and Y_2 respectively. Current liabilities as percentage of total liabilities were varying widely in Bokiyu Tanneries. The maximum proportion was at

75.34 per cent in the year Y_5 and the minimum was at 30.40 per cent in the year Y_2. India Precision Bearings had an increasing trend in the proportion of current liabilities to total debt. It was at about 12.83 per cent in the year Y_1 and reached to 38.52 per cent in the year Y_4. However, this proportion had never increased beyond 40 per cent and had been by and large stable. In the years Y_5 and Y_6 the ratio was 11.33 per cent and 19.51 per cent respectively.

Coromandal Pharma always had more than 10 per cent proportion of current liabilities to total debt except in the year Y_1 where it was 4.71 per cent. It gradually increased from 4.71 per cent in the year Y_1 to 36.50 per cent in the year Y_4.

Mico Farm Chemicals had a continuously increasing proportion of current liabilities to total debt from the year Y_o onwards. The proportion was at 13.37 per cent in the year Y_o and reached a maximum of 63.88 per cent in the year Y_5. This proportion had been less than 40 per cent till the year Y_3 and suddenly jumped to 58.55 per cent by the very next year, that is Y_4.

Sivamani Spinning had a ratio of 23.71 per cent in the year Y_{-2}. However, it had crossed about 75 per cent by the year Y_2, reached to a maximum of 76.95 per cent by the year Y_3 and declined slightly to 74.58 per cent by the year Y_4.

It may be concluded that the proportion of current liabilities in the total debt is to the extent of about 40 per cent for a majority of the sample units in many years. This implies that the role of current liabilities is very significant and managing them with proper care would benefit the companies.

9. DECOMPOSITION ANALYSIS

In this section, it is now proposed to study the decomposition of the items of total current assets and total current liabilities for the years of the post-takeover. This analysis would reveal how each item of the current assets and current liabilities has changed during the post-takeover period.

9.1. Dempo Dairy: Table - 2.10 presents a picture of the decomposition of current assets. As mentioned earlier, there has been a continuous increase in the total assets. The trend in inventories was stable except for the year y_2, where it was at 23.28 per cent. Same trend could be observed with regard to cash and bank balances, wherein, the proportion of cash and bank balances to total current assets is at about 29 per cent. That means there has been an excess of almost 10 per cent cash and bank balances in the year Y_2. Since this yields no return or less return, the idle cash would have affected the profitability of the company. Receivables are more or less stable at an average of about 50 per cent. There had been no investments from the year Y_2 onwards, though there were excess cash balances.

Table - 2.10: Decomposition of the Current Assets of Dempo Dairy after the Takeover

(In percentages)

Items \ *Years*	Y_0	Y_1	Y_2	Y_3
Inventories	39.13	31.65	23.28	31.93
Receivables	56.52	48.10	47.62	50.42
Investments	2.17	1.27	Nil	Nil
Cash & Bank Balances	2.18	18.99	29.10	17.65
I. Total Current Assets	100.00 (46.00)	100.00 (79.00)	100.00 (189.00)	100.00 (238.00)
II. Total Current Liabilities*	(66.00)	(56.00)	(110.00)	(94.00)
II. Net Working Capital	(-20.00)	(23.00)	(79.00)	(144.00)

Notes: Figures within parentheses are absolute amounts in lakh of rupees.
* Break-up of current liabilities was not available.

As regards, current liabilities, there were huge amounts of current liabilities before the takeover and the current liabilities have been less than current assets after the takeover. Further there was an increase in the year Y_2 in the amount of current liabilities.

9.2. ICML: Table – 2.11 presents a view of decomposition of the current assets in the post-takeover period. Though, there

Table - 2.11: Decomposition of the Current Assets and Current Liabilities of ICML after the Takeover

(In percentages)

Items \ Years	Y_0	Y_1	Y_2	Y_3	Y_4
Inventories	40.64	35.86	35.18	27.56	21.06
Sundry Debtors	26.22	15.63	37.92	28.89	22.27
Cash & Bank Balances	0.06	1.48	0.10	21.18	27.03
Loans & Advances	33.08	47.03	26.80	22.37	29.64
I. Total Current Assets	100.00 (47.37)	100.00 (570.57)	100.00 (470.10)	100.00 (575.36)	100.00 (682.50)
Loans (Current)	7.16	19.41	20.58	7.35	Nil
Sundry Creditors (Goods)	19.58	27.21	19.95	17.60	20.91
Sundry Creditors (Service)	46.12	40.05	44.83	51.54	61.73
Trade Credit	3.84	2.27	Nil	Nil	Nil
Customer Credit Balances	6.76	3.07	4.37	13.30	7.73
Other Current Liabilities	16.54	7.99	10.27	10.21	9.63
II. Total Current Liabilities	100.00 (210.63)	100.00 (356.95)	100.00 (275.29)	100.00 (282.55)	100.00 (297.52)
III. Net Working Capital	(-163.26)	(213.62)	(194.81)	(292.81)	(384.98)

Note: Figures within parentheses are absolute amounts in lakh of rupees.

has been a steady increase in the amount of current assets the proportion of inventories to the total current assets has been steadily decreasing in the post-takeover period. Sundry debtors were maximum at 37.92 per cent in the year Y_2. The cash and bank balances were nominal in the years Y_0, Y_1 and Y_2. But they were 21.18 per cent and 27.03 per cent in the years Y_3 and Y_4 respectively. The loans and advances were high at 47 per cent in the year Y_1 and they had been stabilised around 25 per cent in the subsequent years. The drastic reduction in loans and advances in the year Y_2 by about 20 per cent had resulted in the over all reduction of total current assets.

As can also be seen from Table - 2.11 the items of the current liabilities also show a stable trend. Sundry creditors for goods had been around 20 per cent. Sundry creditors for services had been mostly between 40 per cent and 50 per cent, with an exception of year Y_4, where it was 61.73 per cent. There was no trade credit after year Y_2 and customer credit balances were at an average of 5 per cent except for the year Y_3. The other current liabilities have been stable at around 10 percent in the post-takeover period. On the whole, the fluctuations in the current assets and current liabilities are not many over the study period.

9.3. Amar Dye-Chem: The proportion of individual items of the current assets of this company, as seen in Table - 2.12, are stable with minor variations. The inventories were maintained between 45 per cent and 50 per cent. Similarly, sundry debtors were around 40 per cent. Cash and bank balances were between 1 to 2 per cent. However, the loans and advances component is showing an increasing trend and is fluctuating between 5.94 per cent in the year Y_0 and 13.22 per cent in the year Y_2.

As shown in Table 2.12, in the current liabilities and provisions, there were only three major heads: sundry creditors, short-term loans and provisions. All the remaining heads were very insignificant with negligible proportions. The sundry creditors had been maintained between 25 per cent in the post-takeover period and the provisions were at about 10 per cent. Short-term loans had been between 60 and 65 per cent in the post-takeover period. It may be concluded that both current assets and current liabilities are having stable trends in case of Amar Dye-Chem.

Table - 2.12: Decomposition of the Current Assets and Current Liabilities of Amar Dye - Chem after the Takeover

(In percentages)

Items \ *Years*	Y_0	Y_1	Y_2
Inventories	48.93	48.31	44.48
Sundry Debtors	43.17	41.80	41.20
Cash and Bank Balances	1.96	0.94	1.10
Loans & Advances	5.94	8.95	13.22
I. Total Current Assets	100.00	100.00	100.00
	(3510.30)	(3150.42)	(2682.90)
Sundry Creditors	43.85	28.48	25.89
Other current liabilities	0.76	0.60	0.49
Provisions	12.49	10.12	8.62
Loans (Current)	42.90	60.80	65.00
II. Total Current Liabilities	100.00	100.0	100.00
	(3956.63)	(4902.70)	(5646.27)
III. Net Working Capital	(-446.33)	(-1752.28)	(-2963.37)

Note: Figures within parentheses are absolute amounts in lakh of rupees.

9.4. **Bokiyu Tanneries:** The significant components of this company's current assets are: Inventory, Sundry Debtors and Loans and Advances as can be seen from Table - 2.13. Inventories have recorded a declining trend in their proportion in the post-takeover period except for the year Y_5. Interestingly, the sundry debtors had recorded an opposite trend to Inventories. Their proportion had been increasing from year Y_1 (17.56 per cent) to Y_4 (69.30 per cent). There were frequent fluctuations with increase and decrease in the proportion of loans and advances. The cash and bank balances and other current assets were in nominal proportions, without any major changes.

Table - 2.13: Decomposition of the Current Assets and Current Liabilities of Bokiyu Tanneries after the Takeover

(In percentages)

Items \ *Years*	Y_0	Y_1	Y_2	Y_3	Y_4	Y_5
Inventories	57.72	65.33	54.30	42.09	16.77	25.05
Sundry Debtors	27.48	17.56	34.76	53.31	69.30	63.55
Cash & Bank Balances	0.55	1.26	1.57	1.73	1.29	2.07
Other Current Assets	0.04	0.01	0.02	0.01	Nil	Nil
Loans & Advances	14.21	15.84	9.35	2.86	12.64	9.33
I. Total Current Assets	100.00 (70.39)	100.00 (180.61)	100.00 (246.98)	100.00 (464.63)	100.00 (1341.21)	100.00 (1879.12)
Sundry Creditors	24.98	25.92	31.76	58.00	56.44	64.35
Advances from parties	16.72	0.28	0.22	0.19	Nil	Nil
Other liabilities	11.39	8.32	8.86	6.00	31.35	23.74
Interest accrued but not due on loans	0.77	0.10	6.28	3.00	0.24	0.06
Loans (current)	46.14	65.38	52.88	32.81	11.97	11.85
II. Total Current Liabilities	100.00 (205.92)	100.00 (283.71)	100.00 (327.27)	100.00 (399.70)	100.00 (1078.15)	100.00 (1691.98)
III. Net Working Capital	(-135.53)	(-103.10)	(-80.29)	(64.93)	(263.06)	(187.14)

Note: Figures within parentheses are absolute amounts in lakh of rupees.

In the current liabilities as shown in Table 2.13, sundry creditors, advances from parties short-term loans, and other liabilities occupied significant proportions. Sundry creditors did not follow any trend with frequent increases and decreases. However, the advances from parties were at 16.72 per cent in the year Y_0 and subsequently, they became insignificant till year

Y_3. Later from year Y_4 onwards there were no advances from parties. Other liabilities were fluctuating very widely with steep increases and decreases. Short-term loans were also in great proportions with a maximum of 65.38 per cent in the year Y_1 and a minimum of 11.85 per cent in the year Y_5. They were continuously declining from year Y_1 to Y_5. On the whole, this company did not have any stability in the proportions of current assets and current liabilities.

9.5. India Precision Bearings: From Table - 2.14, it can be seen that the total current assets of this unit were continuously increasing except for the years Y_3 and Y_6, where they had declined. The inventory had been mostly more than 60 per cent during the study period. Sundry debtors were generally on an increasing proportion. The proportion of loans and advances were on a declining trend. However, the cash and bank balances had been very widely fluctuating between a high of 6.40 per cent and a low of 0.78 per cent. These balances were less than 1 per cent in the years Y_1 and Y_2. Subsequently, they had slightly improved.

Table - 2.14: Decomposition of the Current Assets of India Precision Bearings after the Takeover

(In percentages)

Years / *Items*	Y_0	Y_1	Y_2	Y_3	Y_4	Y_5	Y_6
Inventories	62.69	57.66	68.31	68.27	69.82	63.86	59.07
Sundry Debtors	11.30	19.08	18.74	19.48	21.19	27.26	28.25
Cash & Bank Balances	6.40	0.78	0.90	1.99	2.87	4.08	3.92
Loans & Advances	19.61	22.48	12.05	10.26	6.12	4.80	8.76
I. Total Current Assets	100.00 (318.00)	100.00 (340.42)	100.00 (507.88)	100.00 (477.82)	100.00 (546.91)	100.00 (741.80)	100.00 (718.54)
II. Total Current Liabilities*	(325.65)	(202.49)	(512.51)	(605.76)	(683.18)	(217.83)	(308.42)
III. Net Working Capital	(-7.65)	(137.93)	(-4.63)	(-127.94)	(-136.27)	(523.97)	(410.12)

Notes: Figures within parentheses are absolute amounts in lakh of rupees.

* Break-up of current liabilities was not available.

9.6. Coromandal Pharma: In this company, the current assets were not showing any steady trend (Table - 2.15). Of the current liabilities, only sundry creditors, short-term loans and other liabilities occupied significant proportions. Though there were advances for suppliers, creditors for other finances and interest accrued they were not present in all the years of the post-takeover period. There was a declining trend in case of sundry creditors and an increasing trend in case of other liabilities.

Table - 2.15: Decomposition of the Current Assets and Current Liabilities of Coromandal Pharma after the Takeover

(In percentages)

Items \ Years	Y_0	Y_1	Y_2	Y_3	Y_4
Inventory	2.47	31.04	48.60	30.04	7.27
Sundry Debtors	53.76	0.47	33.20	9.00	7.64
Cash & Bank	5.84	38.27	0.51	14.10	20.17
Balances Loans & Advances	37.93	30.22	17.69	46.86	64.92
I. Total Current Assets	100.00 (8.91)	100.00 (42.81)	100.00 (94.77)	100.00 (202.31)	100.00 (318.40)
Sundry creditors	6.26	74.19	25.65	20.31	15.38
Other Liabilities	2.86	11.53	15.78	21.45	23.45
Interest Accrued but not due	Nil	Nil	Nil	3.99	2.10
Creditors for other finances	1.71	0.94	0.19	Nil	Nil
Advances for suppliers	Nil	7.61	2.27	Nil	Nil
Loans (current)	89.17	5.73	56.11	54.25	59.07
II. Total Current Liabilities	100.00 (113.23)	100.00 (16.93)	100.00 (82.70)	100.00 (118.12)	100.00 (293.64)
III. Net Working Capital	(-104.32)	(25.88)	(12.07)	(84.19)	(24.76)

Note: Figures within parentheses are absolutes amounts in lakh of rupees.

As can be seen from Table - 2.15, short-term loans were at a high proportion of 89.17 per cent in the year Y_0 and dropped suddenly to 5.73 per cent in the very next year. However, it was maintained steadily between 55 per cent and 60 per cent in the subsequent years.

To conclude, finally, this company also does not have any trend in the proportions of current assets and current liabilities.

9.7. Mico Farm Chemicals: In this company, inventories, sundry debtors, cash and bank balances, and loans and advances occupied significant proportions in the current assets over the study period Table - 2.16. Nevertheless, there had been

Table - 2.16: Decomposition of the Current Assets and Current Liabilities of Mico Farm Chemicals after the Takeover

(In percentages)

Items \ *Years*	Y_0	Y_1	Y_2	Y_3	Y_4	Y_5
Inventory	54.85	37.06	27.73	33.30	18.97	21.36
Sundry Debtors	21.36	45.91	54.85	56.53	72.16	55.56
Cash & Bank Balances	15.52	5.99	6.82	2.38	0.31	6.53
Other Current Assets	0.08	0.13	0.15	0.16	0.01	5.94
Loans & Advances	8.19	10.91	10.45	7.63	8.55	10.61
I. Total Current Assets	100.00 (193.39)	100.00 (379.44)	100.00 (543.47)	100.00 (534.48)	100.00 (910.59)	100.00 (1000.60)
Loans (current)	Nil	43.68	51.78	29.25	51.03	48.34
Sundry Creditors	38.55	14.05	18.04	32.50	30.00	23.32
Other liabilities	48.86	36.66	27.28	36.04	16.89	21.91
Interest accrued but not due on loans	4.05	2.19	1.03	0.88	0.31	0.23
Provisions	8.54	3.42	1.87	1.33	1.77	6.20
II. Total Current Liabilities	100.00 (58.54)	100.00 (146.49)	100.00 (268.10)	100.00 (267.89)	100.00 (623.29)	100.00 (695.88)
III. Net Working Capital	(134.85)	(232.95)	(275.37)	(266.59)	(287.30)	(304.72)

Note: Figures within parentheses are absolute amounts in lakh of rupees.

frequent increases and decreases in the proportion of inventories. Thus there was no clear trend in this. However, sundry debtors had a steady trend with regular increases. It had started with a proportion of 45.91 per cent in the year Y_1 and ended with 72.16 per cent in the year Y_4.

In the current liabilities and provisions, sundry creditors, other liabilities, short-term loans and provisions were in significant proportions in current liabilities as is evident from Table 2.16. Sundry creditors were having a mixed trend with frequent increases and decreases over the period of study. Other liabilities also had been on a mixed trend with regular decreases and increases. The provisions and Interest accrued but not due on loans did not have a steady trend. Short-term loans were between 40 per cent and 50 per cent in all the years of the post-takeover except in the year Y_3.

9.8. Sivamani Spinning: In the case of Sivamani Spinning also the total current assets had been on an increasing trend and were steadily increasing (Table 2.17). The inventories were less than 40 per cent in the year Y_{-2}, but had increased to more than 50 per cent in the year Y_2 and Y_3. However, this had come down again to about 45 per cent in the year Y_4. The sundry debtors were less than 40 per cent in the years Y_2 and Y_3 and more than 40 per cent in the years Y_2 and Y_4. Loans and advances were about 15 per cent in the year Y_{-2} but came down to around 5 per cent in the post-takeover period. Cash and bank balances were a little over 2 per cent in the years Y_3 and Y_4. It was very low in the year Y_2 at 0.02 per cent.

Table - 2.17: Decomposition of the Current Assets and Current Liabilities of Sivamani Spinning after the Takeover

(In percentages)

Items \ Years	Y_{-2}	Y_{-1}	Y_0	Y_1	Y_2	Y_3	Y_4	Y_5
Inventory	38.35	NA	NA	NA	50.99	55.54	45.35	NA
Sundry Debtor	34.18	NA	NA	NA	43.65	37.18	48.13	NA

(Contd...)

Cash and Bank Balances	7.02	NA	NA	NA	0.02	2.10	2.52	NA
Loans & Advances	15.59	NA	NA	NA	5.34	5.18	4.00	NA
Other Current Assets	4.86	NA	NA	NA	Nil	Nil	Nil	Nil
I. Total Current Assets	100.00 (12.96)	NA NA	NA NA	NA NA	100.00 (123.23)	100.00 (165.69)	100.00 (247.96)	NA NA
Sundry creditors	63.99	NA	NA	NA	Nil	Nil	Nil	NA
Unsecured loans	25.36	NA	NA	NA	Nil	Nil	Nil	NA
Other current liabilities	10.65	NA	NA	NA	Nil	Nil	Nil	NA
Liabilities for Cap. Exp.	Nil	NA	NA	NA	0.05	0.05	0.06	NA
Liabilities for Purchase	Nil	NA	NA	NA	19.83	21.47	38.70	NA
Liabilities for Expenses	Nil	NA	NA	NA	6.12	9.89	11.32	NA
Liabilities for other finance	Nil	NA	NA	NA	25.56	23.58	30.81	NA
Liabilities for Bank O.D.	Nil	NA	NA	NA	3.87	3.93	4.76	NA
Loans (Current)	Nil	NA	NA	NA	44.57	41.08	14.35	NA
II. Total Current Liabilities	100.00 (67.36)	NA NA	NA NA	NA NA	100.00 (385.04)	100.00 (374.77)	100.00 (321.95)	NA NA
III. Net Working Capital	(-54.40)	NA	NA	NA	(-261.81)	(-209.08)	(-73.99)	NA

Note: Figures within parentheses are absolute amounts in lakh of rupees.

From Table – 2.17, a complete shift can be seen in the structure of current liabilities from the pre-takeover period to the post-takeover period. However, the amount of current liabilities had been steadily increasing. It was Rs. 67.36 lakh in the year Y_{-2} and reached to Rs. 312.95 lakh by the year Y_4.

On analysis of the items of current assets and current liabilities, it may be concluded that inventories and receivables have occupied higher proportions in current assets and sundry creditors has occupied high proportion among current liabilities in the sample units.

10. ANALYSIS OF SOURCES AND USES STATEMENTS AND DIVERSION OF FUNDS

Besides ratios, there are other measures of liquidity like Cash Budgets and Sources and Uses Statements. A Cash Budget is useful to know whether a firm faces a genuine problem of meeting its cash payments in the near future, whereas the sources and uses statement tells how the firm got into current liquidity situation from its previous position.

The sources and uses statement identifies the major changes in sources and uses of financing that have occurred, during the period, from the year of the takeover to the latest year for which accounting data is available. Any increase in a liability or decrease in an asset is a source of funds, whereas an increase in an asset or a decrease in a liability is taken as a use of funds.

Firms face liquidity problems mainly because of the use of short-term liabilities in financing fixed assets. As a result of this, when a short-term debt becomes due, no cash will have been generated by the asset and the firm may face severe financial distress. The use of short-term sources of funds, for long-term purposes can be extremely unhealthy for any firm. Unfortunately, this type of situations is not uncommon in Indian Corporate Sector. Therefore, the Sources and Uses Statement can identify the inappropriate financing practices that could have led to the firm's liquidity problems. Now, let us analyse this on a company basis. In this study comparative statements of sources and uses for each company have been prepared for the year of takeover (Y_o) and the latest year for which data were available after the takeover (Y_n). From Tables – 2.18 to 2.25, it can be verified that the net change in sources and uses of total assets between the years Y_o and Y_n is exactly the same as the difference between the balances of assets for the years Y_o and Y_n. Similarly, the difference in the total liabilities between the years Y_o and Y_n is also exactly equal to the net change in sources and uses of liabilities for the years Y_o and Y_n. However, in this analysis the main thrust is on finding the total sources and uses of funds and their diversion from the year Y_o to Y_n, and not on finding the net changes. Hence, the net change has not been shown in the presented data. In the following pages the company-wise analysis of sources and uses of funds between the years Y_o and Y_n are presented.

10.1. Dempo Dairy: In this case a comparison of sources and uses of funds is made for the years Y_o and Y_3 in Table - 2.18.

Table - 2.18: Changes in Sources and Uses of Funds between the Years Y_o and Y_3 of Dempo Dairy

(Rs. in lakh)

Items	*Years* Y_o	Y_3	*Sources*	*Uses*
Inventories	18.00	76.00	-	58.00
Receivables	26.00	120.00	-	94.00
Investments	1.00	Nil	1.00	-
Cash & Bank Balances	1.00	42.00	-	41.00
Total Current Assets	46.00	238.00		
Fixed Assets	223.00	157.00	66.00	-
Total Assets	269.00	395.00		
Current Liabilities	66.00	94.00	28.00	-
Long Term Liabilities	723.00	464.00	-	259.00
Net Worth	-520.00	-163.00	357.00	-
Total Liabilities	269.00	395.00	452.00	452.00

Diversion of Funds:

(Rs. in lakh)

	Long-term	*Short-term*		*Total*
Sources	423.00	29.00	=	452.00
Uses	259.00	193.00	=	452.00
	164.00	-164.00		

Rs. 164.00 lakh of long-term funds have been diverted for short-term uses.

From Table - 2.18, it can be seen that there has been an increase in all the current assets and current liabilities. However, the fixed assets and long-term liabilities decreased, from the level of year Y_0, in the year Y_3. During the period Y_0 and Y_3, the major source of funds is from the decline in the negative balance of net worth. Current liabilities and fixed assets also provided some funds during this period. The major user of funds in this period was long-term liabilities in addition to current assets. On the whole, the long-term sources have provided Rs. 423.00 lakh of funds and used only Rs. 259.00lakh. On the other hand, the short-term sources have provided Rs. 29.00 lakh and used Rs. 193.00 lakh during the period Y_0 and Y_3. In other words, there has been a diversion of Rs. 164.00 lakh of long-term funds for short-term uses.

10.2. ICML: In this case, a comparison of sources and uses of funds is made between the year of takeover (Y_0) and the latest year for which accounts are prepared (Y_4) in Table - 2.19.

Table - 2.19: Changes in Sources and Uses of Funds between the Years Y_0 and Y_4 of ICML

(Rs. in lakh)

Items	*Years* Y_0	Y_4	*Sources*	*Uses*
Inventories	19.25	143.74	-	124.49
Sundry Debtors	12.42	152.02	-	139.60
Cash & Bank Balances	0.03	184.50	-	184.47
Loans & Advances	15.67	202.23	-	186.56
Total Current Assets	47.37	682.49		
Fixed Assets	72.62	68.16	4.46	-
Investments	0.51	0.02	0.49	-
Total Assets	120.50	750.67		

(Contd...)

Current Liabilities				
Borrowings from Banks	15.08	Nil	-	15.08
Sundry Creditors-goods	41.25	62.21	20.96	-
Sundry Creditors-Services	97.15	183.66	86.51	-
Trade Deposits	8.10	Nil	-	8.10
Customer Credit Balance	14.23	23.00	8.77	-
Other liabilities	34.82	28.64	-	6.18
	210.63	297.51		
Long-Term Liabilities	473.17	709.30	236.13	-
Net Worth	-563.30	-256.14	307.16	-
Total Liabilities	120.50	750.67	664.48	664.48

Diversion of Funds:

(Rs. in lakh)

	Long-term	*Short-term*		*Total*
Sources	548.24	116.24	=	664.48
Uses	Nil	664.48	=	664.48
	548.24	-548.24		

Rs. 548.24 lakh of long-term funds have been used for short-term purposes.

There has been an increase in the use of current assets. Long-term assets provided little source of funds and the net worth of the company has increased to Rs. -256.14 lakh from Rs. -563.30 lakh. This increase had provided a source of funds to the extent of Rs. 307.16 lakh. On the whole, the long-term sources provided Rs. 548.24 lakh of funds, whereas the short-term sources provided only Rs. 116.24 lakh and used an amount of Rs. 664.48 lakh. The excess funds used for short-term purposes are from long-term sources. This means that the funds raised from long-term sources are used to finance a portion of short-term uses. This diversion of funds is a healthy practice, as suggested by many expert committees including the Tandon Committee.

10.3. Amar Dye - Chem: As already stated, this company was taken over in the year 93-94 (Y_0) hence, there are data available for only two years (Y_1 and Y_2). Therefore, the comparison is made between Y_0 and Y_2 in Table - 2.20.

In this case, there has been a decline in most of the current and fixed assets and a decrease in long-term liabilities. However, the net worth has become negative at Rs. -1,975.27 lakh in year Y_2 from a positive figure of Rs. 72.83 lakh. The long-term sources have provided only Rs. 307.18 lakh but have used up Rs. 2,824.22 lakh. This means that the long-term purposes have used Rs. 2,517.04 lakh more than what they could generate. However, the short-term sources have generated Rs. 2,946.05 lakh but used only Rs. 429.01 lakh. The balance of Rs. 2,527.04 lakh has been diverted by the company for long-term uses impairing liquidity.

Table - 2.20: Changes in Sources and Uses of Funds between the Years Y_0 and Y_2 of Amar Dye-Chem

(Rs. in lakh)

	Years			
Items	Y_0	Y_2	*Sources*	*Uses*
Inventories	1,717.42	1,193.25	524.17	-
Sundry Debtors	1,515.35	1,105.28	410.07	-
Cash & Bank Balances	68.97	29.44	39.53	-
Loans & Advances	208.56	354.93	-	146.37
Total Current Assets	3,510.30	2,682.90		
Fixed Assets	1,297.04	989.86	307.18	-
Investments	210.38	210.38	-	-
Total Assets	5,017.72	3,883.14		

(Contd...)

Sundry Creditors	1,735.06	1,461.79	-	273.27
Interest Accrued but Not Paid	1.16	0.23	-	0.93
Other Current Liabilities	28.69	27.71	-	0.98
Provisions	1,697.56	3,669.84	1,972.28	-
Loans (current)	494.16	486.70	-	7.46
Total Current Liabilities	3,956.63	5,646.27		
Long-Term Liabilities	988.26	212.14	-	776.12
Net Worth	72.83	-1,975.27	-	2,048.10
Total Liabilities	5,017.72	3,883.14	3,253.23	3,253.23

Diversion of Funds:

(Rs. in lakh)

	Long-term	*Short-term*		*Total*
Sources	307.18	2,946.05	=	3,253.23
Uses	2,824.22	429.01	=	3,253.23
	-2,517.04	2,517.04		

Rs. 2,517.04lakh of short-term funds have been used for long-term purposes.

10.4. Bokiyu Tanneries: In this case, a comparison has been made, of the sources and uses, for the years Y_0 and Y_5 in Table - 2.21.

Table - 2.21: Changes in Sources and Uses of Funds between the Years Y_0 and Y_5 of Bokiyu Tanneries

(Rs. in lakh)

	Years			
Items	Y_0	Y_5	*Sources*	*Uses*
Inventories	40.63	470.79	-	430.16
Sundry Debtors	19.34	1,194.21	-	1,174.87

(Contd...)

Cash & Bank Balances	0.39	38.84	-	38.45
Other Current Assets	0.02	Nil	0.02	-
Loans & Advances	10.00	175.27	-	165.27
Total Current Assets	70.38	1,879.12		
Fixed Assets	20.88	381.69	-	360.81
Total Assets	91.26	2,260.81		
Sundry Creditors	51.44	1,077.81	1,026.37	-
Advance from Parties	34.44	Nil	-	34.44
Other Liabilities	23.45	397.56	374.11	-
Interest Accrued but Not Paid	1.58	1.06	-	0.53
Provisions	Nil	15.00	15.00	-
Loans (Current)	95.00	200.55	105.55	-
Total current liabilities liabilities	205.91	1,691.98		
Long-term Loan Funds	192.45	179.06	-	13.39
Net Worth	-307.10	389.77	696.87	-
Total Liabilities	91.26	2,260.81	2,217.92	2,217.92

Diversion of Funds:

(Rs. in lakh)

	Long-term	*Short-term*		*Total*
Sources	696.87	1,521.05	=	2,217.92
Uses	374.20	1,843.72	=	2,217.92
	322.67	-322.67		

Rs. 322.67 lakh of long-term funds have been used for short-term purposes.

There had been an increase in the current and fixed assets. Even the current liabilities and loan funds had increased. But the net worth had improved drastically from Rs. -307.10 lakh in the year Y_0 to Rs. 389.77 lakh, making a total source of Rs. 696.87 lakh of sources of funds. On the whole, the total long-term sources provided an amount of Rs. 696.87 lakh and used only Rs. 374.20 lakh. However, the short-term sources were Rs. 1,521.05 lakh but used up Rs. 1,843.72 lakh. This implies that there had been an additional use of Rs. 322.67 lakh of long-term sources of funds for short-term uses.

10.5. India Precision Bearings: A comparison of sources and uses of funds has been made for the years Y_0 and Y_6 of this company in Table - 2.22.

Table - 2.22: Changes in Sources and Uses of Funds between the Years Y_0 and Y_6 of India Precision Bearings

(Rs. in lakh)

Items	Years		Sources	Uses
	Y_0	Y_6		
Inventories	199.37	424.42	-	225.05
Sundry Debtors	35.92	203.01	-	167.09
Cash & Bank Balances	20.34	28.17	-	7.83
Loans & Advances	62.37	62.94	-	0.57
Total Current Assets	318.00	718.54		
Fixed Assets	653.18	862.64	-	209.46
Total Assets	971.18	1,581.18		
Current Liabilities	160.42	271.06	110.64	-
Loans (current)	165.23	37.36	-	127.87
Loan Funds	1,316.57	1,546.24	229.67	-
Net Worth	-651.61	-265.69	385.92	-
Miscellaneous Exp.	-19.43	-7.79	11.64	-
Total Liabilities	971.18	1,581.18	737.87	737.87

Diversion of Funds:

(Rs. in lakh)

	Long-term	*Short-term*		*Total*
Sources	627.23	110.64	=	737.87
Uses	209.46	528.41	=	737.87
	417.77	-417.77		

Rs. 417.77 lakh of long-term funds have been used for short-term purposes.

There had been an increase in all the current assets and fixed assets, thus became the major user of funds. Further there was a decline in the current loans to the extent of Rs. 127.87 lakh. Similarly, there had been increases in the current liabilities and long-term loan funds. Further, the net worth had provided an amount of Rs. 385.92 lakh by reducing the negative net worth to that extent. All these could turn out to be good sources of funds. On the whole, long-term sources had provided Rs. 627.23 lakh but used up Rs. 209.46 lakh only. On the other hand, the short-term sources provided only Rs. 110.64 lakh and used Rs. 528.41 lakh. This implies that the excess funds of Rs. 417.77 lakh used for short-term purposes had come from long-term sources. Therefore, there was a diversion of Rs. 417.77 lakh of funds from long-term sources to short-term uses.

10.6. Coromandal Pharma: A comparison of sources and uses has been made, in this company, for the years Y_0 and Y_4 in Table - 2.23.

Table - 2.23: Changes in Sources and Uses of Funds between the Years Y_0 and Y_4 of Coromandal Pharma

(Rs. in lakh)

	Years			
Items	Y_0	Y_4	*Sources*	*Uses*
Inventories	0.22	23.16	-	22.94
Sundry Debtors	4.79	24.32	-	19.53

(Contd...)

Cash & Bank Balances	0.52	64.22	-	63.70
Loans & Advances	3.38	206.70	-	203.32
Total Current Assets	8.91	318.40		
Fixed Assets	98.39	561.48	-	463.09
Investments	Nil	0.39	-	0.39
Total Assets	107.30	880.27		
Sundry Creditors	7.08	45.17	38.09	-
Other liabilities	3.24	68.87	65.63	-
Creditors for Others' Finances	1.94	Nil	Nil	1.94
Interest Accrued but Not Paid	Nil	6.15	6.15	-
Loans (Current)	100.97	173.45	72.48	-
Total Current Liabilities	12.26	293.64		
Loan Funds	303.16	909.83	606.67	-
Miscellaneous Exp.	-0.17	-78.96	-	78.79
Net Worth	-308.92	-244.24	64.68	-
Total Liabilities	107.30	880.27	853.70	853.70

Diversion of Funds:

(Rs. in lakh)

	Long-term	*Short-term*		*Total*
Sources	671.35	182.35	=	853.70
Uses	542.27	311.43	=	853.70
	129.08	-129.08		

Rs. 129.08 lakh of long-term funds have been used for short-term purposes.

There had been an increase in current assets and fixed assets. Also there was an increase in current liabilities and loan funds. However, the net worth, though negative, improved from year Y_0 to Y_4, and thereby provided a source of funds. In this case, investments are not treated as current assets since these have not been included under the heading current assets. Similarly, miscellaneous expenditure under liabilities has not been shown under current liabilities for a similar reason. The company had generated an amount of Rs. 671.35 lakh from long-term sources and used only Rs. 542.27 lakh. The funds generated from short-term sources were Rs. 182.35 lakh and the funds used were Rs. 311.43 lakh. This implies that there has been a diversion of funds from long-term sources to short-term uses to the extent of Rs. 129.08 lakh.

10.7. Mico Farm Chemicals: In this case, the comparison of sources and uses of funds has been done between the years Y_0 and Y_5 in Table - 2.24.

Table - 2.24: Changes in Sources and Uses of Funds between the Years Y_0 and Y_5 of Mico Farm Chemicals

(Rs. in lakh)

Items	*Years*		*Sources*	*Uses*
	Y_0	Y_5		
Inventories	106.07	213.76	-	107.69
Sundry Debtors	41.31	555.90	-	514.59
Cash & Bank Balances	30.02	65.35	-	35.33
Other Current Assets	0.16	59.39	-	59.23
Loans & Advances	15.83	106.20	-	90.37
Total Current Assets	193.39	1,000.60		
Fixed Assets	115.19	196.33	-	81.14
Total Assets	308.58	1,196.93		
Sundry Creditors	22.57	162.12	139.55	-
Interest Accrued but not Paid	2.37	1.57	-	0.80
Other Current Liabilities	28.60	152.34	123.74	-

(Contd...)

Provisions	5.00	43.49	38.49	-
Borrowing from Banks	Nil	336.36	336.36	-
Total Current Liabilities	58. 54	695.88		
Loan Funds	379.33	393.49	14.16	-
Net Worth	-129.29	107.56	236.85	-
Total Liabilities	308.58	1,196.93	889.15	889.15

Diversion of Funds:

(Rs. in lakh)

	Long-term	*Short-term*		*Total*
Sources	251.01	638.14	=	889.15
Uses	81.14	808.01	=	889.15
	169.87	-169.87		

Rs. 169.87 lakh of long-term funds have been used for short-term purposes.

In this company also, there has been increases in current and fixed assets and current liabilities and loan funds. There was a negative net worth in the year Y_0 at Rs. -129.29 lakh and it had become positive and increased to Rs. 107.56 lakh by year Y_5. This item alone has provided an amount of Rs. 236.85 lakh as a source of funds. On the whole the long-term sources have provided Rs. 251.01 lakh of funds against a use of Rs. 81.14 lakh. The short-term sources have provided Rs. 638.14 lakh of funds and used up Rs. 808.01 lakh. This means, there has been a diversion of funds from long-term sources to short-term uses to the extent of Rs. 169.87 lakh.

10.8. Sivamani Spinning: In this case, a comparison has been made between year Y_{-2} and Y_4 in Table - 2.25, as data for Y_0 and Y_5 were not available, as stated earlier.

There has been an increase in all the items of current assets. This had been the major user of funds. Further, there was a decline in the long-term liabilities and increase in negative net worth of the unit, thereby using the funds. The major sources of funds were from decrease in the fixed assets and increase in the current liabilities. On the whole, the long-term sources had generated Rs. 131.53 lakh and used Rs. 151.12 lakh during the study period. On the other hand, the short-term sources had generated Rs. 255.23 lakh from various sources but used only Rs. 235.64 lakh, thus providing a surplus of Rs. 19.59 lakh. This surplus had been used for long-term purposes.

Table - 2.25: Changes in Sources and Uses of Funds between the Years Y_{-2} and Y_4 of Sivamani Spinning

(Rs. in lakh)

Items	*Years* Y_{-2}	*Years* Y_4	*Sources*	*Uses*
Inventories	4.97	112.44	-	107.47
Receivables	4.43	119.35	-	114.92
Cash & Bank Balances	0.91	6.26	-	5.35
Loans & Advances	2.02	9.92	-	7.90
Others	0.63	Nil	0.63	-
Total Current Assets	12.96	247.97		
Fixed Assets	228.83	97.30	131.53	-
Investments	Nil	0.01	-	0.01
Total Assets	241.79	345.28		
Current Liabilities	67.35	321.95	254.60	-
Long Term Liabilities	216.76	109.71	-	107.05
Net Worth	-42.32	-86.38	-	44.06
Total Liabilities	241.79	345.28	386.76	386.76

Diversion of Funds:

(Rs. in lakh)

	Long-term	*Short-term*		*Total*
Sources	131.53	255.23	=	386.76
Uses	151.12	235.64	=	386.76
	-19.59	19.59		

Rs. 19.59 lakh of short-term funds have been used for long-term purposes.

Basing on the above analysis, the sample units can be categorized into two groups, as:

1. Companies where funds from long-term sources are put to short-term uses like:
   - (a) Dempo Dairy
   - (b) ICML
   - (c) Bokiyu Tanneries
   - (d) India Precision Bearing
   - (e) Coromandal Pharma
   - (f) Mico Farm Chemicals
2. Companies where funds from short-term sources are put to long-term uses such as:
   - (a) Amar Dye-Chem
   - (b) Sivamani Spinning

From the above it is evident that a majority (6 out of 8) of the sample companies have used the long-term sources of funds for short-term purposes, and thus could achieve better standards of liquidity.

11. FINDINGS

The study started with a hypothesis that there is an improvement in the liquidity position of the sample units after the takeover. The hypothesis is verified with the help of certain standard ratios and funds flow analysis. The findings against the stated hypothesis are as follows:

1. All the companies except Amar Dye-Chem had better current ratios in the post-takeover period, when a comparison is made between the post and the pre-takeover periods. Amar Dye-Chem has more than 1:1 ratio before the takeover and it had been sharply declining in the post-takeover period. This implies that the company is gradually losing its liquidity. In almost all the cases, current ratio has been more than 1:1 in many of the years in the post-takeover. In some cases the ratio

has been as high as 3.30:1. Ideally, the companies should maintain a ratio of around 2:1. In the present study, most of the companies are not able to reach the general standard even in the post-takeover period.

2. As far as quick ratio is concerned, the sample companies are showing three types of trends:

a. Companies with increasing quick ratio after the takeover,

b. Companies with a mixed trend i.e. some times increasing and sometimes decreasing quick ratio in the post-takeover, and

c. Companies with declining quick ratio. Generally, all the companies have a better quick ratio in the post-takeover period. However, India Precision Bearings had a declining and low quick ratio till the year Y_4 and Sivamani Spinning also had a low but increasing quick ratio in the post-takeover period.

On the whole, the following 6 of the 8 companies have an ideal quick ratio of 1:1 in at least one or more of the years of the study period:

1. Dempo Dairy
2. ICML
3. Bokiyu Tanneries
4. India Precision
5. Coromandal Pharma
6. Mico Farm Chemicals

3. Absolute liquid assets are at nominal levels in almost all the companies even after the takeover.

4. There had been mostly negative net working capital in all the companies before the takeover. All the companies except Amar Dye-Chem, and Sivamani Spinning have turned around after the takeover and their net working capital turned out to be positive for many years during the post-takeover period. In case of Amar Dye-Chem and Sivamani Spinning the net working capital continues to be negative even after the takeover. One can see a clear and marked shift in the trend of net working capital towards positive direction during the takeover period. A synoptic view presented below proves this point:

Name of the Company	*C.R. of Y_n (times)*	*Q.R. of Y_n (times)*	*NWC of Y_n (Rs. in lakhs)*
Dempo Dairy	2.53	1.72	144.00
ICML	2.29	1.81	384.98
Amar Dye-Chem	0.48	0.26	-2963.37
Bokiyu Tanneries	1.11	0.83	187.14
India precision	2.33	0.95	410.12
Coromandal Pharma	1.08	1.01	24.76
Mico Farm Chemicals	1.44	1.13	304.72
Sivamani Spinning	0.77	0.42	-73.99

It can be seen from the above table that six companies have a current ratio of more than 1:1 and two companies have less than 1:1 ratio. They are, Amar Dye-Chem and Sivamani Spinning.

Similarly, going by the quick ratio criteria, these very six companies have a ratio of 0.5:1, which is comparatively a reasonable ratio in the context of the present study. In terms of NWC criteria also the same six companies registered positive net working capital and the remaining two with negative net working capital. This measurement also tells that the above six units only are liquid and the remaining two are illiquid. Therefore, it may be concluded that all the three measurements of liquidity, viz., current ratio, quick ratio and net working capital have revealed the similar results and that the above 6 companies have adequate liquidity.

5. Measured in terms of cash flows, except Amar Dye-Chem, all the sample companies have negative net cash flows in the per-takeover period. All the companies (excepting

Coromandal Pharma) could turnaround by the year Y_n and convert negative cash flows into positive figures. In contrast, Amar Dye-Chem, which had positive net cash flow in the year $Y_{'0}$ yielded negative net cash flows after the takeover.

6. With respect to operational liquidity (computed using net cash flows and current liabilities), only one company, i.e., Dempo Dairy had more than a hundred per cent of operational liquidity in the year Y_3. Excepting this, no other company had adequate operational liquidity. Since all the companies of the sample were sick and are in the process of turnaround after the takeover, most of the companies do not have operational liquidity of even 40 per cent for majority of the years of the study period.

7. The proportion of quick assets to current assets is mostly more than 50 per cent in majority of the companies which means that the inventories constitutes less than 50 per cent of the total current assets. The proportion of current assets to total assets also has been mostly more than 50 per cent in most of the sample companies, which shows the dominant role of current assets in the asset structure of the sample units. The proportion of quick assets in the total assets is mostly between 30 and 40 per cent. The proportion of current liabilities to total debt has been less than 40 per cent for a majority of the years.

8. The decomposition analysis of current assets and current liabilities, revealed the fact that the inventories and the receivable occupied high proportions in the total of current assets and sundry creditors occupied high proportion among current liabilities.

9. The analysis of sources and uses of funds has led to the conclusion that in a majority of the sample companies, long-term funds have been used for short-term purposes. Interestingly, increase in the net worth

Of the companies has been a constant source of funds in a majority of the companies. In case of two companies, viz., Amar Dye-Chem and Sivamani Spinning, there was a diversion of short-term funds for long-term purposes. It is suggested by many financial experts that a portion or the permanent portion of working capital (short-term funds) has to be financed through permanent or long term sources of funds for better liquidity. Going by this principle, it may be concluded that the following units have better liquidity when a comparison is made between the year of takeover (Y_o) and the latest year for which financial data has been made available (Y_n). The companies are:

1. Dempo Dairy
2. ICML
3. Bokiyu Tanneries
4. India Precision Bearings
5. Coromandal Pharma
6. Mico Farm Chemicals

The following are the companies, which have lost their liquidity from year Y_o to year Y_n.

1. Amar Dye-Chem
2. Sivamani Spinning

It may be concluded that the above companies are using short-term funds for long-term uses. This is happening because of the reason that the companies are not able to raise funds from long-term sources. When this kind of diversion takes place there is all the likelihood of illiquidity and thereby not honouring the dues, which leads to many problems.

REFERENCES

1. Archer, S.H. and D' Ambrosio, C.A. (1972), *Business Finance - Theory and Management*, The Macmillan Company, New York, p. 445.
2. Firth, Michael (1976), *Management of Working Capital*, The Macmillan Press Ltd., London 1976, p. 122. Also see K.A.Menon , (1977), "Liquidity of the Indian Corporate Sector", *Reserve Bank Staff Occasional Papers*, Vol.2, No.1, June.
3. James McNeill Stancill (1987), *Harvard Business Review*, March-April, 1987.

4. Van Horne, James C. (1995), *Financial Management and Policy*, Prentice-Hall of India Pvt. Ltd., New Delhi, pp.361.

5. Rao, K.V. (1990), *Management of Working Capital in Public Enterprises*, Deep & Deep Publications, New Delhi.

6. Walter, James E. (1957), 'Determination of Technical Solvency', *The Journal of Business*, Vol. xxx, No.1, January, pp. 30-43. Reprinted in J.L. O' Downell and M.S. Goldberg (Eds.), *Elements of Financial Administration*, op. cit., pp. 73-91.

7. *Ibid.*, pp. 73-91.

8. Bierman, H. (1960), "Measuring Financial Liquidity," *The Accounting Review* xxx v, October, pp. 628-32.

9. Benston, G. and G.H. Sorter (1960), "Appraising the Defensive Position of A Firm - The Interval Measure", *The Accounting Review*, xxxv, October, pp. 33-40.

10. Parashar, S.P. (1986), *Liquidity Management - Principles and Practice of Managing Cash Flow*, Vision Books Pvt. Ltd, New Delhi.

11. Lamke, K.V. (1970), "The Evaluation of liquidity - An analytical study", *Journal of Accounting Research*, Spring, pp. 44-77.

12. Parashar, S.P., (1986), *op. cit.*

13. Spiller, E.A., Homewood, Ill. *Financial Accounting*, (1977), Richard D. Irwin, p. 644.

14. Archer, S.H. and D' Ambrosio, C.A. (1972), *Business Finance - Theory and Management*, The Macmillan Company, New York, p. 449.

Chapter III

LEVERAGE ANALYSIS

In this chapter an attempt has been made to study the changes in leverage of the sample units from the pre-takeover to the post-takeover period.

1. HYPOTHESIS

The changes in leverage should result in better solvency, and thereby lead to better liquidity and profitability as a result of the takeover.

2. LEVERAGE ANALYSIS - THEORETICAL FRAMEWORK

In order to increase the profits, companies may seek different ways of conducting business. In this context considerable attention is given to the issues pertaining to leverage. The type of leverage is assumed to have a direct bearing on the profitability of the enterprise. Several authors have emphasized the leverage aspect through the study of relationships between the Earnings Before Interest and Taxes (EBIT) and the Earnings Per Share (EPS). A dictionary meaning of the term 'leverage' would refer to 'an increased means of accomplishing some purpose'.

"In some cases, as with lifting heavy objects, leverage allows one to accomplish things not otherwise possible at a given level of effort".[1] In the business context, the term leverage may be defined as "the employment of an asset or source of fund for which the firm has to pay a fixed cost or fixed return".[2] The finance manager can identify different types of leverage and in most cases; the effects are reversible, so that the leverage may be favourable or unfavourable.

2.1. Types of Leverage

Leverage can be categorised into three types as given below:

1. Operating Leverage
2. Financial Leverage, and
3. Combined Leverage

Operating leverage depends on the company's operating fixed costs. These are the fixed costs other than the interest on debt. These include costs like administrative expenses, depreciation, advertising expenditure and property taxes. On the other hand, financial leverage depends on financial fixed costs like interest expenses, loan fees, etc.; combined leverage is an attempt to provide a total measure of both operating and financial leverages. In other words, "leverage associated with investment (asset acquisition) activities is referred to as operating leverage; while leverage associated with financing activities is called financial leverage".[3]

Operating leverage is determined by the relationship between the firm's sales revenues and its EBIT or operating profits. Whereas, financial leverage represents the relationship between the firm's EBIT and earnings available to the equity shareholders. Thus, EBIT or operating profit is used as the pivotal point in defining operating and financial leverages. In a way, operating and financial leverage represent two stages in the process of determining the earnings available to the equity shareholders.

2.1.1. Operating Leverage: Operating leverage may be defined as the firm's ability to use fixed operating costs to magnify the effects of changes in sales on EBIT. Operating leverage results from the existence of fixed operating expenses in the firm's income stream. The operating costs of a firm fall into three categories, viz., (i) Fixed Costs; (ii) Variable Costs; and (iii) Semi-Variable Costs. However, in operational terms, the third category, i.e. Semi-Variable Costs rarely exist; as it can be broken down into fixed and variable components. Operating leverage occurs whenever a firm incurs fixed costs that must be met regardless of volume. Companies employ assets with fixed cost in the hope that volume will produce revenues more than sufficient to cover all fixed and variable costs. Operating Leverage is measured in precise way in terms of Degree of Operating Leverage (DOL). DOL measures in quantitative terms the extent of degree of Operating Leverage. The greater the DOL, the higher the Operating Leverage. The following equation is used to compute operating leverage:

$$\text{DOL} = \frac{\text{Percentage Change in Net Operating Income or EBIT}}{\text{Percentage Change in Sales}}$$

Operating leverage tells the impact of changes in sales on operating income. If a firm has a high degree of operating leverage, even a small change in sales has large effects on EBIT. If there is a small rise in sales, profits will rise drastically and if there is a small decline in sales, EBIT may be wiped out and a loss may be reported. Therefore, firms prefer to operate sufficiently above break-even to avoid the damage that may be caused owing to low sales. This is because, firms do not operate under conditions of high degree of operating leverage, as it is highly risky and a small drop in sales can be excessively damaging to the firm's efforts in achieving the profitability.

2.1.2. Financial Leverage: It may be defined as the "ability of a firm to use fixed financial charges to magnify the effects of changes in EBIT on the firm's earnings per share"[4]. In other words; financial leverage involves the use of funds obtained at a fixed cost in the hope of increasing the return to the shareholders. The sources from which a firm can raise funds for long-term uses are: Long-term Debt and Equity.

Presence of debt capital, which carries fixed financial

charges, in the capital structure of a firm, is a delicate issue. Comparing the ROI made on the assets with the interest payments assesses the impact of debt on the profitability of a firm. The underlying assumption is that the fixed charge funds (debt) can be obtained at a cost lower than the company's rate of return on its assets. It gives an opportunity to the shareholders to get additional earnings without increasing their investment and, consequently, the EPS or the return on equity will increase.

On the other hand, failure to earn a higher return than the cost of borrowed funds and greater use of borrowed funds without considering the earnings capacity would only result in equity erosion. Thus Financial Leverage not only tends to magnify returns under favourable conditions but also exposes the firms to financial risk. The greater the degree of financial leverage, the wider will be the fluctuations in the return on equity.

Financial leverage can be expressed precisely in terms of Degree of Financial Leverage (DFL) and it is calculated by using the following equation:

$$\text{DFL} = \frac{\text{Percentage Change in Net Income}}{\text{Percentage Change in EBIT}}$$

2.1.3. Combined Leverage: Since both Operating and Financial Leverages are closely concerned with ascertaining the firm's ability to cover fixed charges, if we combine them both, the result is Total Leverage and the risk associated with combined leverage is known as Total Risk. Combined Leverage can be analysed in terms of Degree of Combined Leverage (DCL) and it is symbolically expressed as:

$$\text{DCL} = \text{DOL} \times \text{DFL}$$

$$= \frac{\text{Percentage Change in EBIT}}{\text{Percentage Change in Sales}} \times \frac{\text{Percentage Change in Net Income}}{\text{Percentage Change in EBIT}}$$

$$= \frac{\text{Percentage Change in Net Income}}{\text{Percentage Change in Sales}}$$

Thus, the DCL measures the percentage change in EPS due to percentage change in sales. The combined leverage can work in both directions. It will be favourable, if sales increase and unfavourable when sales decrease.

2.2. Leverage Ratios

Leverage in the finance literature is also studied with the help of certain ratios. These ratios are categorised into three broad groups as indicated below:

1. Ratios Relating to Capital Structure
2. Ratios Relating to the Impact of Leverage on Liquidity
3. Ratios Relating to the Impact of Leverage on Profitability

2.2.1. Capital Structure Ratios

Ratios relating to the capital structure are classified into two sub-groups as:

i. Ratios, which are based on the relationship between the borrowed funds and owner's funds like:
   1. Debt to Equity Ratio
   2. Total Debt to Total Asset Ratio
   3. Equity to Total Assets Ratio
   4. Total Debt and Equity to Total Assets Ratio

ii. Ratios calculated from Profit and Loss Account. These are popularly known as coverage ratios. These include the following:
   a. Interest Coverage Ratio
   b. Dividend Coverage Ratio
   c. Total Fixed Charges Coverage Ratio

d. Cash flow Coverage Ratio

e. Debt Service Coverage Ratio

Besides the above, several authors have used several other ratios in their attempt to comprehend the ramifications of leverage. For instance, N.P. Agarwal[5], analysed long-term solvency of the Aluminum Industry through the following ratios:

1. Debt-Equity Ratio
2. Ratio of Capital Gearing
3. Fixed Assets to Net worth Ratio

Capital gearing has been defined by J. Batty,[6], as "the relation of ordinary shares to preference shares and loan capital is described as the capital gearing". The idea behind this ratio is to compare the components in two groups, i.e., funds bearing fixed charges or interest and the other funds from the equity shareholders, which do not bear any fixed charges or fixed dividends. This ratio is calculated by dividing the total of long-term borrowed funds and paid-up preference share capital by the amount of paid-up equity share capital.

In another attempt, G. Prasad and K.V. Rao[7] used the following ratios to study the Capital Structure in the State Level Public Enterprises:

1. Debt-Equity Ratio
2. Debt as a percentage of Net worth
3. Debt as a percentage of Paid-up Capital
4. Interest as a percentage of Gross Profit
5. Interest as a percentage of Total Income

Lawrence D. Schall and Charles W. Haley[8] have also analysed the leverage of firms through the following four ratios:

1. Debt to Total Asset Ratio
2. Debt to Equity Ratio

3. Times Interest Earned
4. Fixed Charges Coverage

While assessing the performance of its assisted units, the Industrial Credit and Investment Corporation of India[9] (ICICI) used the following leverage ratios:

1. Debt to Equity Ratio
2. Net worth as a percentage of Total Net Assets
3. Total Debt as a percentage of Net worth
4. Long-term Borrowings from Financial Institutions as a percentage of Net Fixed Assets.

From the foregone discussion, it may be concluded that the following ratios appear to be most commonly used for measuring the leverage of a firm:

a. Debt to Equity Ratio
b. Total Debt to Total Assets Ratio
c. Equity to Total Assets Ratio
d. Total Debt and Equity to Total Assets Ratio

In the subsequent paragraphs these ratios have been briefly explained.

a. Debt-Equity Ratio: This is an important tool of Financial Analysis to appraise the financial solvency of a firm. It has important implications from the viewpoint of the creditors, owners and the firm itself. This ratio reflects the relative contribution of creditors and owners of business in its financing. A high ratio shows a large share of financing by the creditors in relation to the owners and, therefore, a larger claim against the assets of the firm. A low ratio implies a smaller claim of creditors.

If the Debt-Equity Ratio is high, the owners are putting up relatively less money of their own which is a danger signal for the creditors. If the project fails, the creditors would loose heavily. Moreover, with a small financial stake in the firm, the owners may behave irresponsibly and indulge in speculative activity.

A high Debt-Equity Ratio has equally serious implications from the firm's point of view. A high proportion of debt in the capital structure would lead to inflexibility in the operations of the firm, since creditors would exercise pressure and interfere in management's activities. Secondly, such a firm would be able to borrow only under very restrictive terms and conditions. Further, it would have to face a heavy burden of interest payments, particularly in adverse conditions. Finally, the firm will have to encounter serious difficulties in raising funds in future.

A low debt-equity ratio has just the opposite implications. To the creditors, a relatively high stake of equity implies sufficient margin of safety and substantial protection against shrinkage in assets. For the company also, the servicing of debt is less burdensome and consequently its credit standing is not adversely affected, its operational flexibility is not in jeopardy and it will be able to raise additional funds. Nevertheless, the shareholders of the firm are deprived of the benefits of trading-on-equity or leverage.

From the above discussion, one can understand that both high and low debt-equity ratio situations are not desirable. There should be a proper balance of debt and equity. There is no rule as to the ideal proportion of debt and equity. The proportion is dependent upon various factors. Financial experts favoured a ratio of 2:1 between the debt and equity. The guidelines issued under the erstwhile Capital Issues (Control) Act, 1947, fixes a ratio of 2:1 and a higher ratio are being considered on merits of certain types of capital-intensive industries.[10]

b. Total Debt to Total Assets Ratio: This ratio measures the proportion of total debt to total assets. The total debt comprises long-term debt and current liabilities. This ratio measures the share of the total assets financed by outside funds. Generally, creditors prefer a low ratio, as it implies a greater protection of their proportion. A higher ratio generally means that the firm must pay a higher rate on its borrowings and its interest burden would be more. Beyond a point, the firm may not be able to borrow funds at all. Hence, this ratio should be at reasonable levels, depending upon the firm's position.

c. Equity to Total Assets: This ratio indicates the proportion of total assets financed through the equity capital. Here, equity denotes only equity capital and it does not include any reserves or retained earnings. Generally, owners would like to invest less when the company is either in losses or when the debt is cheaper. The owners try to bring more of their money when the company is in good profits or the debt is costlier. The higher the proportion of equity to total assets, the lower the interest burden on the company. As a general rule, companies use equity only when the debt financing is difficult or costly.

d. Total Debt and Equity to Total Assets Ratio: This ratio tells us what proportion of total assets is financed through the total debt and equity put together. In a healthy unit, the total assets shall be more than the amount of total debt and equity. The excess portion of the assets are normally, financed by reserves and surpluses of the companies accumulated over a period of time. However, there could be firms, which have total assets equal to or less than the total of debt and equity. Situations of this type arise when there are no reserves and surpluses and accumulated losses are in significant proportion.

It may be inferred from the above that if a firm's total debt and equity put together are less than 1 time of the total assets, then it is a healthy company with reserves and surpluses covering the remaining portion of the total assets. On the contrary, if a firm's total debt and equity are more than 1 time of the total assets, then the firm is not a healthy one and the excess portion of the total debt and equity should have been used against the accumulated losses.

2.2.2. Leverage and Liquidity

James. C.,[11] Van Horne. Has suggested the following ratios to measure the impact of leverage on liquidity:

1. $$\frac{PBT + I + DEP}{\text{Total Debt}}$$

2. $$\frac{PBT + I + DEP}{\text{Long-term Debt}}$$

3. $$\frac{\text{Total Borrowings + Equity}}{PBT + I + DEP}$$

A measure of the ability of a company to service its debt is the relationship of annual cash flow to the amount of debt outstanding. The cash flow of a company has been defined in this context as Profit Before Tax + Interest + Depreciation.

In this study it has been termed as Earnings Before Interest, Taxes and Depreciation (EBITD). In order to keep the terms used in the above ratio in tune with the terms used in the study the notations are rewritten as follows:

a. $$\frac{EBITD}{\text{Total Debt}}$$

b. $$\frac{EBITD}{\text{Long-term Debt}}$$

c. $$\frac{\text{Total Borrowings + Equity}}{EBITD}$$

These ratios are particularly helpful in corporate restructuring, where heavily leveraged transactions occur. They have proven their usefulness in predicting the deteriorating financial health of a company.

2.2.3. *Leverage and Profitability*

G. Prasad and K.V. Rao[12], while studying the capital structure in State Level Public Enterprises have suggested three ratios to study the impact of leverage on profitability. They are:

1. Interest Coverage Ratio
2. Interest as a Percentage of Total Income
3. Interest as a Percentage of Gross Profits

All the above three ratios compare interest, which is a cost of debt, with different concepts and attempts to judge the effect of leverage on profitability. Each of these ratios is explained in the subsequent paragraphs hereunder:

a. Interest Coverage Ratio

This ratio is one of the most traditional ratios among the leverage ratios. It is a simple ratio of EBIT to the interest charges. This ratio is used to test the firm's debt-servicing capacity and tells, by how many times the interest charges are covered by the funds generated from operations. Generally, a higher ratio is desirable, but too high a ratio indicates that the firm is very conservative in using debt. A lower ratio indicates either an excess use of debt or lesser EBIT owing to inefficient operations.

b. Interest as a percentage of Total Income

This ratio reveals the proportion of interest to total income and how it has changed over time during the study period. The higher the proportion, the greater the burden on the company's profits. Therefore, it needs to be at reasonable levels. A higher proportion of interest may occur due to the following reasons:

i. Presence of higher debt in the capital structure of the firm,

ii. Higher rate of interest, and

iii. Low total income generated

Under normal conditions, total income should increase, when the funds are borrowed and put into the business. Higher amount of interest should be followed by higher total income and thereby maintain this ratio at a reasonable level.

c. Interest as a percentage of Gross Profits

This ratio is an attempt to relate the interest with the gross profit. In other words, this ratio attempts to study the firm's ability to meet the first and immediate obligation after meeting the cost of goods sold. Interest is a fixed obligation and the surplus, after meeting the cost of goods sold, has to be utilised first to meet this obligation. Therefore, this ratio is a refined measure of knowing the impact of debt on the profitability.

An interest percentage of 100 to the gross profit mean that the firm has just the sufficient gross profit to meet its interest obligations. Therefore, the guiding principle in this ratio could be, if the percentage is more than a hundred per cent, the firm is not healthy.

ANALYSIS OF LEVERAGE

After carefully analysing the above, it has been decided to use the following leverage ratios, besides studying degrees of leverage, to study the leverage aspects of the firms included in the study.

An attempt has been first made to study the degrees of leverages for the years Y_o - Y_1 and Y_{n-1} - Y_n and compare them to identify the changes over the study period. This is followed by the ratio analysis from the point of view of leverage. These ratios have been divided into three broad categories as shown below:

(i) Capital structure ratios

(ii) Ratios showing the impact of capital structure on liquidity of the firm and

(iii) The ratios showing the impact of capital structure on the profitability of the firm

With the help of these ratios the changes and trends in the leverage are studied. Finally, an analysis also had been done in order to study the pattern of and changes in financing of assets from the year Y_o to Y_n to underline the impact of leverage on the sample units.

3. DEGREES OF LEVERAGE

A perusal of Table - 3.1, which shows the comparison of financial leverage, operating leverage and combined leverage of the sample units for the years Y_o-Y_1 (the change between the first year of takeover and the year of takeover) and Y_{n-1} -Y_n (the change between the latest year for which accounting data is available and the year pervious to it) reveals the fact that most of the sample units have negative values for the variables used in the computation of degrees of leverage.

TABLE - 3.1: A Comparison of Degrees of Leverage of Sample Units between the Years Y_o - Y_1 and Y_{n-1} - Y_n

	Degrees of Leverage					
	Y_o - Y_1			*Y_{n-1} - Y_n*		
Company	*FL*	*OL*	*CL*	*FL*	*OL*	*CL*
Dempo Dairy	-	-	-	3.62	1.15	4.16
ICML	-	-	-	-	-	-
Amar Dye-Chem	-	-	-	-	-	-
Bokiyu Tanneries	-	-	-	-	-	-
India Precision	2.19	0.36	0.79	2.35	0.02	0.05
Coromandal Pharma	5.37	-	-	4.77	-	-
Mico Farm	0.80	0.48	0.39	0.86	-	-
Sivamani Spinning	-	-	-	-	-	-

Note: '-' Indicates negative values. 'FL' indicates Financial leverage, 'OL' indicates operating leverage and 'CL' indicates combined leverage.

The following are some of the observations in this regard.

(i) In the year Y_o-Y_1, there were 3 companies, out of the sample 8, which had a positive financial leverage, but the operating and combined leverages were positive for only 2 out of 8 units.

(ii) In the year Y_{n-1} - Y_n, there was positive leverage for 4 units in respect of financial leverage. However, the operating leverage and the combined leverage were positive in only two cases.

(iii) Only one unit, i.e. India Precision Bearings, had all positive leverages both in the years Y_o-Y_1 and Y_{n-1} - Y_n.

As there were mostly negative leverages, this method of assessing leverage does not appear to be much meaningful to draw any reliable conclusion. As such, the study depended on the analysis of leverage through ratios.

4. RATIOS RELATING TO CAPITAL STRUCTURE

In this section, the ratios relating to capital structure have been studied in order to bring out the changes over the study period. The ratios used for measuring these structural changes are:

a. Debt to Equity Ratio

b. Total Debt to Total Assets Ratio

c. Equity to Total Assets Ratio

d. Total Debt and Equity to Total Assets Ratio

4.1. Debt to Equity Ratio

In the present study, a relationship between the long-term debt and equity has been established. This ratio was lower and generally declining in the post-takeover period in a majority of the sample units. As can be seen from Table 3.2, the ratio was the lowest at 0.09 times for the year Y_2 in case of Amar Dye-Chem and the highest at 8.34 times in case of Dempo Dairy for the year Y_1. There have been fluctuations in this ratio for all the sample units from year to year.

The following is the unit-wise analysis of this ratio:

Table - 3.2: Debt to Equity Ratio of Sample Units

(Times)

Companies \ Years	Y_{-4}	Y_{-3}	Y_{-2}	Y_{-1}	Y_0	Y_1	Y_2	Y_3	Y_4	Y_5	Y_6
Dempo Dairy	2.36	3.35	3.24	5.19	7.61	8.34	5.39	4.88	NA	x	x
ICML	NA	NA	NA	NA	4.92	3.50	3.01	3.07	3.09	x	x
Amar Dye-Chem	4.55	3.53	3.52	3.49	0.44	0.28	0.09	x	x	x	x
Bokiyu Tanneries	0.15	0.15	0.16	1.21	3.86	4.56	5.43	5.95	5.10	3.39	x
India Precision	1.98	2.65	2.82	3.26	4.39	4.58	4.30	4.03	3.63	5.68	5.15
Coromandal Phar	NA	NA	NA	8.45	8.59	2.73	2.27	1.09	1.18	x	x
Mico Farm Chem	NA	NA	NA	7.25	5.62	7.09	5.53	5.44	4.67	4.16	x
Sivamani Spinning	2.52	2.75	3.00	NA	NA	NA	1.31	1.12	1.10	NA	x

Notes: 'NA' Indicates Data not available.,'X' Indicates the years beyond year Y_n.

Dempo Dairy had a maximum debt in the year Y_1, and hence, there had been a highest Debt to equity ratio in that year. However, in the subsequent years there had been a decline in the long-term debt. There had been no change in the equity over the entire period of study. In the pre-takeover period, there had been huge proportions of current liabilities in the total liabilities, as a result of this; there had been lower levels of Debt to equity ratios in the pre-takeover years.

In the case of ICML, there was an increase in the equity in the year Y_1 from Rs. 96.13 lakh to Rs. 227.82 lakh. Though, the Debt to equity ratio in the year Y_0 was about 5 times, there was a decline in this ratio from 4.92 times to 3.5 times. Subsequently it had been around 3 times, without any major changes.

Amar Dye-Chem also had enhanced its equity from Rs. 678.44 lakh to Rs. 2233.69 lakh in the year Y_0. Very interestingly, it had an average debt to equity ratio of about 3.5 times in the pre-takeover period but this ratio had suddenly came down to 0.44 times in the year Y_0 and had declined further in the subsequent year and reached to a minimum of 0.09 times in the year Y_2. This was mainly due to an increase in the equity and a drastic decrease in the long-term liabilities.

Bokiyu Tanneries had very less long-term debt in the first 3 years of the study period and thereby very low debt-equity ratio. However, from the year Y_1, it had started improving and reached a maximum of 5.95 times by the year Y_3. But in the subsequent two years this ratio had shown a declining trend and had declined to 3.39 times. It may be noted that there was no change in the amount of equity over the study period.

There was no significant change in the equity of India Precision also. There had been a general increase in the long-term debt. As a result of this, the Debt-Equity ratio had been generally on an increasing trend and was fluctuating in tune with the fluctuations of long-term debt.

Coromandal Pharma had a very high debt-equity ratio of about 8.5 times in years Y_{-1} and Y_0. However, from year Y_1, there had been a declining trend upto year Y_3, where the ratio was 1.09 times and had increased marginally to reach 1.18 times in the year Y_4. Interestingly, there had been a continuous increase in the equity capital in all the years of the study period.

Mico Farm Chemicals had a ratio of about 7 times in the years Y_{-1} and Y_1. However, it had started gradually declining from the year Y_2 and had reached a minimum of 4.16 times by the year Y_5. It can be seen that there had been increases in the equity twice during the study period, viz. in the years Y_0 and Y_2.

Sivamani Spinning had increasing and higher debt-equity ratios in the pre-takeover years. However, in the post- takeover period there had been a declining trend and the ratio was around 1 time from the year Y_2 onwards. An increase in the capital could be seen from year Y_2.

We can now conclude that in the process of turnaround some companies enhanced their equity contribution and some others used the debt financing and 'traded on equity'. The companies that enhanced the equity are:

1. ICML
2. Amar Dye-Chem
3. Coromandal Pharma
4. Mico Farm Chemicals
5. Sivamani Spinning

The companies those depended heavily on debt financing are:

1. Dempo Dairy
2. Bokiyu Tanneries
3. India Precision

Of the sample of eight units four units, viz., Dempo Dairy, Amar Dye-Chem, Mico Farm Chemicals and Sivamani Spinning had a declining ratio in the post-takeover period. The remaining units had a mixed trend in this ratio with frequent increases and decreases. This ratio had been mostly between 3 times and 5 times during the study period, against a standard of 2 times.

4.2. Total Debt to Total Assets Ratio

In the present study, this ratio has been mostly more than 1 time for a majority of the sample units in most of the years. This signifies the fact that the total assets are less than the total debt. This implies high financial risk to the firm. Table-3.3 shows that the ratio of total debt to total assets has fluctuated in this study between the lowest of 0.76 and the highest of 5.67 times. After the takeover, there has been a general decline in the trend of this ratio in all the companies except in Amar Dye-Chem and Coromandal Pharma.

Let us now examine how this ratio has moved in each of the sample companies over the study period.

Dempo Dairy had an increasing trend in this ratio in the period from Y_{-4} to Y_1. However, it had declined from 3.06 times in the year Y_1 to 1.69 times in the year Y_2. The decline was sudden and drastic. There was also a significant increase in the total assets in that year. Both these changes had brought down this ratio drastically. The ratio had showed a declining trend after year Y_1.

ICML had a ratio of less than 2 times in the post-takeover period. However, it had a very high ratio of 5.67 times in the year of the takeover (i.e. Y_0). The decline in this ratio from year Y_0 to Y_1 was quite sharp. The reason for such a drastic decline was that there was more than four- fold increase in total assets, whereas the increase in total debt was less than one time. From year Y_1 onwards the ratio had continuously decreased and reached to a low of 1.34 times by the year Y_4.

Amar Dye-Chem was the only company that had an increasing trend in this ratio, though the increase was marginal. The reason for this was that there had been a gradual increase in the total debt of this company even after the takeover.

There had been a gradual increase in this ratio in the case of Bokiyu Tanneries in the post-takeover period. It was highest

Table - 3.3: Total Debt to Total Assets Ratio of Sample Units

(Times)

Companies \ *Years*	Y_{-4}	Y_{-3}	Y_{-2}	Y_{-1}	Y_0	Y_1	Y_2	Y_3	Y_4	Y_5	Y_6
Dempo Dairy	1.56	1.47	1.70	2.03	2.93	3.06	1.69	1.41	NA	x	x
ICML	NA	NA	NA	NA	5.67	1.80	1.79	1.53	1.34	x	x
Amar Dye-Chem	1.09	1.00	1.00	1.19	0.99	1.25	1.51	x	x	x	x
Bokiyu Tanneries	2.13	2.91	2.97	3.85	4.37	2.24	0.79	0.76	0.76	0.82	x
India Precision	0.99	1.21	1.45	1.57	1.70	1.39	1.28	1.30	1.24	1.19	1.17
Coromandal Pha	NA	NA	NA	3.35	3.88	0.88	1.05	1.04	0.91	x	x
Mico Farm	NA	NA	NA	2.73	1.42	1.24	1.15	1.13	1.00	0.91	x
Sivamani Spin	0.97	1.08	1.18	NA	NA	NA	1.41	1.29	1.25	NA	x

Notes: 'NA' Indicates Data not available.,and 'X' indicates the years beyond year Y_n.

at 4.37 times in the year Y_0. However, in the subsequent year (i.e. Y_1), there had been a sharp decline in this ratio to 2.24 times. It had further declined to 0.79 times in the year Y_2. From the year Y_2 onwards this ratio had stabilised at around 0.80 times, which is a sign of lesser risk and better safety to the outside lenders. Though, there were changes in the years Y_3, Y_4 and Y_5 in the total debt and total assets, the changes were almost in the same proportion and thereby had not effected the ratio significantly.

India Precision, though had an increasing trend in this ratio before the takeover, it had generally a declining ratio after the takeover. However, the changes in the total assets and total debts were marginal and the ratio had fluctuated within the narrow margin of 0.99 times and 1.70 times over the study period. This implies that there had been no change in the risk of outside lenders and the risk had been by and large stable.

Coromandal Pharma had a ratio of more than 3 times in the post-takeover years. However, the ratio had dropped to 0.88 times, from the previous year's 3.88 times. In the year Y_2 it had increased to 1.05 times and subsequently, there had been a declining trend. Mico Farm Chemicals had a steadily declining trend in total debt to total assets ratio. It had started during the study period with a highest ratio of 2.73 times in the year Y_{-1} and ended with a lowest ratio of 0.91 times. The ratio was 2.73 times in the year Y_{-1} and had dropped to 1.42 times by the year Y_0 as a result of doubling of the total assets. Sivamani Spinning had showed an increasing trend from the years Y_{-4} to Y_{-2} and a declining trend from years Y_2 to Y_4. Since the data was not available for the years Y_{-1}, Y_0 and Y_1, it may be concluded that the increasing trend of Y_{-4} to Y_{-2} would have continued and reached a maximum and would have again started declining in the years Y_{-1}, Y_0 and Y_1.

From the above discussion the following conclusions emerge with respect to total debt to total assets ratio:

i. There had been a ratio of mostly more than 1 time, implying that the total debt is more than the total assets in many cases.

ii. In the post-takeover period there had been a declining trend in this ratio in case of Dempo Dairy, ICML, Bokiyu Tanneries, India Precision, Coromandal Pharma, Mico Farm Chemicals and Sivamani Spinning, implying that either the debt of these firms was decreasing or the assets of these units were increasing.

iii. The remaining one unit, viz., Amar Dye-Chem had an increasing ratio even in the post-takeover period. This shows the presence of huge amount of debt in the capital structure of this company.

4.3. Equity to Total Assets Ratio

In the present study, most of the sample companies had their equity capital, aggregating to less than 50 per cent of the total assets. Moreover, the ratio of equity to total assets fluctuated between the lowest of 2 per cent and the highest of 87 per cent as is evident from Table 3.4.

Let us now see how this ratio has moved over the years in the sample companies:

Dempo Dairy had a lower equity to total assets ratio in the post-takeover period. However it had increased in the years Y_0 and Y_1 but only to decline again to about 0.25 times in the years Y_2 and Y_3. There had been no equity increase during the entire study period. The reason for higher ratio in the years Y_0 and Y_1 was that there had been a decline in the total assets without any reduction in the equity. This implies that the equity shareholders are relatively at a higher risk during these two years, since lesser assets were covering their equity.

ICML had a very high ratio of 0.80 times in the year of takeover (Y_0). In other words, it had funded about 80 per cent of its total assets from its equity capital only. Since the total assets were less, the proportion was so high. However, the ratio had decreased to about 0.35 times in the subsequent years and was on a declining trend signifying the increase in total assets in a higher proportion to the increase in equity. Amar Dye-

Table - 3.4: Equity to Total Assets Ratio of Sample Units

(Times)

Companies \ Years	Y_{-4}	Y_{-3}	Y_{-2}	Y_{-1}	Y_0	Y_1	Y_2	Y_3	Y_4	Y_5	Y_6
Dempo Dairy	0.24	0.18	0.19	0.24	0.35	0.34	0.26	0.24	NA	x	x
ICML	NA	NA	NA	NA	0.80	0.35	0.42	0.36	0.30	x	x
Amar Dye-Chem	0.12	0.14	0.14	0.21	0.45	0.51	0.58	x	x	x	x
Bokiyu Tanneries	0.63	0.70	0.64	0.60	0.55	0.22	0.77	0.05	0.03	0.02	x
India Precision	0.32	0.33	0.33	0.30	0.31	0.27	0.21	0.21	0.21	0.19	0.19
Coromandal Pha	NA	NA	NA	0.30	0.33	0.31	0.38	0.72	0.87	x	x
Mico Farm Che	NA	NA	NA	0.23	0.22	0.13	0.14	0.14	0.09	0.08	x
Sivamani Sping	0.27	0.30	0.30	NA	NA	NA	0.37	0.35	0.29	NA	x

Notes: 'NA' Indicates Data not available.
'X' Indicates years beyond year Y_n.

Chem had lower equity to total assets ratio in the pre-takeover period and a relatively better ratio in the post-takeover years. The ratio was about 0.50 times in the post-takeover years. This implies that the company was steadily going from bad to worse. The reason for higher ratio in post-takeover years was that there was an increase in equity in the year Y_0 by about 2 times of the pre-takeover level, but total assets were on a declining trend. Both these two factors had boosted this ratio to higher proportions.

Bokiyu Tanneries had a very high ratio of more than 0.60 times in the years of the post-takeover, as the total assets during that period were less. However, in the years Y_1 and Y_2 the total assets had risen to dramatic levels, mostly financed with the loan funds, as there was no increase in the equity of the firm during the study period. The ratio had steadily declined and gone down to negligible levels with 0.02 times in the year Y_5. This had happened as a result of financing total assets with very high proportions of debt.

There had been a steady decline in this ratio in India Precision Bearings in the post-takeover period. This ratio was 0.30 times or more in the pre-takeover years and was about 0.20 times from year Y_2 onwards. The decline in the ratio was owing to gradual increase in the total assets of the company.

Coromandal Pharma had a steadily increasing ratio during the study period. The ratio had suddenly jumped from 0.38 to 0.72 times from the year Y_2 to Y_3. The reason for this was that the equity had more than doubled during that period, whereas the total assets had an increase of about 20 per cent. One interesting observation in this case was that there was an increase in the equity of this company in every year during the study period.

Mico Farm Chemicals had a ratio of little over 0.20 times the post-takeover period and it had further declined from year Y_1 to reach a minimum of 0.08 times in the year Y_6. There was an increase in equity twice during the study period. There were major increases in the total assets in the years Y_1 and Y_4, without any increase in the equity in those years. Consequently, there was a decline in the ratio. Sivamani Spinning had an increasing ratio prior to the takeover and a declining ratio after the takeover.

To conclude, all the companies, except Amar Dye-Chem and Coromandal Pharma had a declining Equity to Total Assets ratio. This signifies that the equity was covered by more total assets and thereby less risk to owners and their funds.

4.4. Total Debt and Equity to Total Assets Ratio

In the present study, all the sample units had a ratio of mostly more than 1 time. This means that most of the companies had an amount of total debt and equity more than the total assets (Table - 3.5).

The following observations can be made from the data presented in Table - 3.5.

(i) The following five of the eight sample units had a declining trend in this ratio after the takeover, thereby meaning that the proportion of total assets is increasing.

  a. Dempo Dairy

  b. ICML

  c. Bokiyu Tanneries

  d. Mico Farm Chemicals

  e. Sivamani Spinning

(ii) Amar Dye-chem. was showing an increasing trend in this ratio after the takeover, thereby meaning that the proportion of total assets is decreasing.

(iii) The following were the two units, which had a mixed trend in the ratio with frequent increases and decreases even in the post-takeover period.

  a. India Precision

  b. Coromandal Pharma

Table - 3.5: Total Debt and Equity to Total Assets Ratio of Sample Units

(Times)

Companies / *Years*	Y_{-4}	Y_{-3}	Y_{-2}	Y_{-1}	Y_{0}	Y_{1}	Y_{2}	Y_{3}	Y_{4}	Y_{5}	Y_{6}
Dempo Dairy	1.80	1.65	1.89	2.27	3.29	3.40	1.95	1.65	NA	x	x
ICML	NA	NA	NA	NA	6.47	2.15	2.22	1.89	1.64	x	x
Amar Dye-Chem	1.21	1.14	1.14	1.84	1.43	1.76	2.08	x	x	x	x
Bokiyu Tanneries	2.76	3.62	3.61	4.45	4.91	2.46	0.85	0.81	0.79	0.84	x
India Precision	1.31	1.54	1.78	1.87	2.00	1.66	1.49	1.51	1.45	1.38	1.36
Coromandal Pha	NA	NA	NA	3.64	4.21	1.19	1.43	1.77	1.49	x	x
Mico Farm Chem	NA	NA	NA	2.95	1.64	1.38	1.29	1.26	1.09	0.99	x
Sivamani Sping	1.23	1.38	1.47	NA	NA	NA	1.78	1.63	1.54	NA	x

Notes: 'NA' Indicates Data not available.
'X' indicates the years beyond year Y_n.

Now, let us analyse the trends in this ratio in each of the sample units and the causes for the same. Individually, Dempo Dairy always had a ratio of more than 1.65 times, during the study period. This means that the company always had less total assets, when compared with the amount of total debt and equity put together. However, this ratio had started declining from the year Y_1 onwards and reached a minimum of 1.65 times by the year Y_3.

In case of ICML the ratio was as high as 6.47 times in the year Y_0. However, it had come down sharply to 2.15 times in the very next year (Y_1). The reason for this sharp decline in one year was due to a four-fold increase in total assets, though the total debt and equity had just doubled. In this case also the proportion of total debt and equity to the total assets was always more than 1.5 times. However, the company had a declining trend in this ratio after the takeover, which is a positive sign of turnaround.

In case of Amar Dye-Chem, this ratio was closer to 1 time in the years Y_{-1}, Y_{-2} and Y_{-3}. However, in the subsequent years it was more than 1.5 times, except in the year Y_0. One could see an increasing trend in this ratio in the post-takeover period. The reasons for this trend were a declining trend in the total assets and an increasing trend in the total debt and equity.

Bokiyu Tanneries had increasing proportions of total assets in the post-takeover period. This increase was so high that the ratio had not only showed a declining trend but also came down to less than 1 time from the year Y_2 onwards.

India Precision had a ratio of 2 in the year Y_0 and had shown a declining trend since then upto the year Y_2. The reason for this declining trend was that there was an increase in total assets, which was more than the increase in total debt. The equity remained without any significant change in the post-takeover period.

Coromandal Pharma had a low proportion of total assets as could be seen from the higher ratio in the years Y_{-1} and Y_0. There had been a sudden fall in this ratio in the year Y_1, where the ratio had come down from the previous year's 4.21 times to 1.19 times. However, in the years Y_2 and Y_3 the ratio had shown an increasing trend before finally dropping down to 1.49 times in the year Y_4. The reason for the sudden decline in this ratio in the year Y_1 was that there was a four-fold increase in total assets, with total debt at more or less similar level.

Mico Farm Chemicals had a ratio of about 3 times, in the year Y_{-1}. However, it had decreased subsequently to 1.64 times in the next year and had continued to decline thereafter to reach 0.99 times in the year Y_5. The reason for the sudden decline in this ratio in the year Y_0 was that the rate of increase in the total assets was more than the rate of increase in the total debt. Therefore, there had been a decline in this ratio in the post-takeover period. Sivamani Spinning had an increasing ratio in the pre-takeover years and decreasing trends in the post-takeover years.

In a healthy company, as stated earlier, this ratio would always be less than 1 time. However, in the present study, as seen from the foregone discussion, this ratio had been mostly more than one, thus implying the total assets are less than the total debt and equity put together. However, in the post-takeover period this ratio had been generally declining in case of Amar Dye-chem, ICML, Bokiyu Tanneries, India Precision, Coromandal Pharma, Mico Farm Chemicals and Sivamani Spinning.

5. IMPACT OF LEVERAGE ON LIQUIDITY

In this section, an attempt has been made to study the impact of leverage on liquidity of the sample units in the pre and the post-takeover periods. The ratios used for this purpose are:

1. EBITD as a percentage of Total Debt
2. EBITD as a percentage of Long-term Debt
3. Total Debt and Equity to EBITD Ratio

An analysis of the above ratios is made here under:

5.1. EBITD as a Percentage of Total Debt

This ratio relates the EBITD (cash flows) to total debt of the firm, in percentages. This ratio tells the percentage of total debt covered by EBITD. In other words, this ratio tells what proportion of total debt could be repaid with the EBITD of a particular year. The higher the ratio, the better the company's liquidity position.

In the present study, Table 3.6 shows that this ratio had fluctuated between the lowest of 10 per cent and the highest of 30 per cent. This ratio was highest at 30.13 per cent in case of Bokiyu Tanneries in the year Y_3 and lowest at 1.45 per cent in case of Coromandal Pharma in the year Y_2. Out of the eight sample units, six were having positive ratios in the post-takeover period.

The following is a detailed analysis of the sample companies:

In case of Dempo Dairy, this ratio had been mostly less than 10 per cent. In the year Y_0 there was no positive EBITD, hence no ratio. However, in the post-takeover period the ratio had started with 6.37 per cent and continued to increase to 28.32 per cent by the year Y_3.

ICML also had a negative EBITD in the year Y_0 and thereby no ratio. However, in the very next year, Y_1, the ratio was 11.97 per cent. This increasing trend had continued till the next year and subsequently, started declining. In this case this ratio had been mostly less than 15 per cent. Amar Dye-Chem, though, had some positive EBITDs in the pre-takeover period; there were no EBITDs after the takeover. Bokiyu Tanneries did not have positive EBITDs in most of the pre-takeover years; however, there had been all positive EBITDs in the post-takeover period. This ratio had fluctuated between the lowest of 10 per cent and the highest of 30 per cent in the post-takeover period.

India Precision had negative values in EBITD for the first three years of the study in the pre-takeover period. However, the trend had changed and started showing positive EBITDs

Table - 3.6: EBITD as a Percentage of Total Debt of the Sample Units

(In percentages)

Companies \ *Years*	Y_{-4}	Y_{-3}	Y_{-2}	Y_{-1}	Y_0	Y_1	Y_2	Y_3	Y_4	Y_5	Y_6
Dempo Dairy	17.38	4.97	2.12	6.10	+	6.37	14.15	28.32	NA	x	x
ICML	NA	NA	NA	NA	+	11.97	20.07	14.60	12.52	x	x
Amar Dye-Chem	9.16	10.44	11.03	+	20.25	+	+	x	x	x	x
Bokiyu Tanneries	+	+	1.14	+	+	15.04	24.31	30.13	24.26	8.10	x
India Precision	+	+	+	1.93	7.49	13.19	12.59	8.66	4.15	11.61	13.00
Coromandal Pharma	NA	NA	NA	+	+	+	1.45	+	+	x	x
Mico Farm Chem	NA	NA	NA	+	+	12.52	13.10	17.81	17.71	25.28	x
Sivamani Spining	NA	NA	NA	NA	NA	NA	17.01	21.54	10.75	NA	x

Notes: 'NA' Indicates Data not available.,'X' Indicates the years beyond year Y_n.,
'+' Indicates years where the EBITD is negative.

from the year Y_{-1} onwards. Coromandal Pharma had no positive EBITDs even after the takeover period, except for the year Y_2. Consequently, this ratio had not been calculated.

Mico Farm Chemicals had positive EBITDs from the year Y_1. Therefore, this ratio had been calculated from year Y_1. This ratio had been gradually increasing during the post-takeover period except in the year Y_4. This increasing trend in this ratio was mainly due to increasing EBITDs. On the whole, this company had better ratios after the takeover and thereby implying turnaround. Sivamani Spinning had an increasing trend in the years Y_2 and Y_3. However, the ratio had declined to 10.75 per cent from the previous year's 21.54 per cent in the year Y_4. This implied that the company had started with better performance but subsequently, was not able to maintain it.

To sum up, of the eight companies taken up for study, only in case of Dempo Dairy, there was an increasing trend in the ratio, implying an improvement in the liquidity position after the takeover. All the remaining units except Amar Dye-Chem and Coromandal Pharma had exhibited mixed trend with frequent increases and decreases in the ratio. Amar Dye-Chem, though, had a positive ratio in some of the years in the pre-takeover period, had no positive EBITDs and thereby no positive ratios after the takeover. Coromandal Pharma had no positive ratio except for the year Y_2 during the study period.

5.2. EBITD as a percentage of Long-term Debt

This ratio reveals the proportion of earnings before interest, taxes and depreciation to long-term debt. Through this ratio, we would know to what extent long-term debt is covered by EBITD in a particular year. The higher the ratio, the more secure are the long-term debtors.

In the present study, this ratio was ranging between 126.99 per cent and 3.07 per cent during the period of study. The maximum ratio was present in Bokiyu Tanneries and the minimum was in India Precision Bearings. A ratio of a hundred per cent or more implies that the EBITD has covered the entire

Table - 3.7: EBITD as a percentage of Long-term Debt of Sample Units

(Times)

Years / *Companies*	Y_{-4}	Y_{-3}	Y_{-2}	Y_{-1}	Y_0	Y_1	Y_2	Y_3	Y_4	Y_5	Y_6
Dempo Dairy	47.70	12.06	5.77	9.74	+	6.82	22.39	34.05	NA	x	x
ICML	NA	NA	NA	NA	+	17.33	28.12	20.48	17.78	x	x
Amar Dye-Chem	17.65	21.31	22.43	+	101.32	+	+	x	x	x	x
Bokiyu Tanneries	+	+	32.87	+	+	33.80	53.68	70.70	126.99	91.67	x
India Precision	+	+	+	3.07	9.40	15.13	17.59	13.00	23.01	13.10	15.60
Coromandal Pha	NA	NA	NA	+	+	+	7.79	+	+	x	x
Mico Farm Chem	NA	NA	NA	+	+	16.35	19.81	27.09	42.71	70.00	x
Sivamani Spinning	NA	NA	NA	NA	NA	NA	49.17	71.01	42.31	NA	x

Notes: '+' indicates years where the EBITD is negative.
'NA' indicates data not available.
'X' indicates years beyond year Y_n.

long-term debt. Table. 3.7 present a view of this ratio, company-wise, over the study period.

Dempo Dairy had a generally declining ratio in the pre-takeover period. However, this company had a steadily increasing ratio in the post-takeover period. This increasing trend was mainly due to the increasing ratio in the EBITD of the firm in the post-takeover period.

ICML had a positive ratio from the year Y_1 onwards. Though, in the initial years (Y_1 and Y_2) there was an increase in this ratio, subsequently, it was showing a declining trend. The reason for the declining trend was mainly due to declining EBITDs from the year Y_3 onwards.

Amar Dye-Chem as usual had positive ratios in the pre-takeover years and negative ratios after the takeover. Interestingly, this company had a ratio of 101.32 per cent in the year Y_0, which was due to positive EBITD.

Bokiyu Tanneries had negative ratios in the pre-takeover period except for the year Y_{-2}. But after the takeover, this company had ever-increasing ratios. The ratio for the year Y_4 was more than a hundred per cent at 126.99 per cent but had declined to 91.67 per cent in the very next year. However, in the very next year the EBITD had reduced to less than 50 per cent of the previous year. Since, the long-term debt had further declined in the year Y_5, the ratio was at more than 90 per cent, in spite of more than 50 per cent reduction in the EBITD.

India Precision had a positive ratio from the year Y_{-1}. This had gradually increased to 17.59 per cent by the year Y_2 but thereafter it had showed a mixed trend with frequent increases and decreases in the ratio. This trend had been mainly in tune with the trend of EBITD. Coromandal Pharma had a positive ratio only in the year y_2. Mico Farm Chemicals had positive ratio from the year Y_1 after the takeover. There had been a steadily increasing trend after the takeover. This trend had been mainly due to an increasing trend in the EBITDs and a generally declining trend in long-term debt.

Sivamani Spinning had a good ratio of 71 per cent in the year Y_3 and in the remaining two years it had a ratio of 49.17 per cent and 42.31 per cent. Initially, the company had shown an increasing trend but it had declined in the year Y_4.

From the above discussion it could be concluded that two of sample units Dempo Dairy and Mico Farm Chemicals had a steadily increasing trend in the ratio, four units, ICML, Bokiyu Tanneries, India Precision and Sivamani Spinning, had a mixed trend in the ratio with increases and decreases and the remaining two had no positive ratios in the post-takeover period. Therefore, it may be concluded that except these two companies all others had turned around after the takeover and consequently, the ratio had become positive over the study period.

5.3. Total Debt and Equity to EBITD Ratio

This ratio reveals the proportion of total debt and equity to earnings before interest, tax and depreciation. This ratio shows by how many times the total debt and the equity is covered by the EBITD. This ratio gives an idea as to the ability of firm to meet its debt obligation. The lower the ratio the better the ability of the firm to meet its debt and equity obligations. In other words, the lower is the ratio the better would be the liquidity position of the firm. Lenders would be generally conscious of this ratio and they believe that the possibility of default is significant, if this ratio exceeds 8 times.

In the present study, this ratio has varied between the highest of 106 times and the lowest of 4 times. Interestingly both these two figures are present in Bokiyu Tanneries as could be seen from Table 3.8. Let us analyse how this ratio has moved over the study period in each of the sample units.

Dempo Dairy had a high ratio of 47.21 times in the year Y_{-2}. The same had decreased by 50 per cent by the next year, Y_{-1}. However, from the year Y_1 onwards, this ratio had shown a tremendous improvement and reached to 4.13 times by the year Y_3. This ratio, though, showed a mixed trend in the pre-

Table - 3.8: Total Debt and Equity to EBITD Ratio of Sample Units

(Times)

Companies \ Years	Y_{-4}	Y_{-3}	Y_{-2}	Y_{-1}	Y_0	Y_1	Y_2	Y_3	Y_4	Y_5	Y_6
Dempo Dairy	6.64	22.60	47.21	18.37	+	17.46	8.15	4.13	NA	x	x
ICML	NA	NA	NA	NA	+	10.00	6.16	8.44	9.79	x	x
Amar Dye-Chem	12.17	10.90	10.27	+	7.17	+	+	x	x	x	x
Bokiyu Tanneries	+	+	106.62	+	+	7.30	4.46	3.56	4.28	12.67	x
India Precision	+	+	+	61.91	15.69	9.02	9.26	13.46	8.26	9.95	8.93
Coromandal Pharma	NA	NA	NA	+	+	+	93.88	+	+	x	x
Mico Farm Chemicals	NA	NA	NA	+	+	8.85	8.55	6.29	6.15	4.30	x
Sivamani Spinning	NA	NA	NA	NA	NA	NA	7.43	5.90	11.45	NA	x

Notes: '+' indicates years where the EBITD is negative.
'NA' indicates data not available.
'X' indicates years beyond year Y_n.

takeover period, showed a declining trend in the post-takeover period.

ICML had a positive ratio from the year Y_1. This ratio had been always less than 10 times during the study period, though with a mixed trend. Amar Dye-Chem had some positive EBITDs in the pre-takeover years, but all negative EBITDs in the post-takeover period. This ratio had been about 10 times in this case in the pre-takeover period. Bokiyu Tanneries had all negative EBITDs in all the years of the pre-takeover period, except in the year Y_{-2}. This meager EBITD had resulted in a highest ratio of 106.62 times. In the post-takeover period this ratio had been less than 5 times in a majority of the years. The ratio had shown a declining trend upto year Y_3 and showed an increasing trend in the subsequent years. This increasing trend was mainly due to the increase in debt. Therefore, the conclusion emerging was that with increasing doses of debt the liquidity was declining as could be seen from the figures of year Y_4 and Y_5.

India Precision had showed mostly a ratio of less than 10 times, though there had been frequent increases and decreases in the ratio. Coromandal Pharma had all negative EBITDs during the study period except for the year Y_2, where the ratio was as high as 93.88 times.

Mico Farm Chemicals had a steadily declining trend in this ratio in the post-takeover period. It was always less than 10 times and was as low as 4.30 times by the year Y_5. There had been gradual increases in the debt and a stable equity. The EBITD was also regularly increased in tune with the increase in debt but at a higher rate, thereby creating a declining trend in this ratio. This was an evidence of getting better liquidity with increase in the debt. In other words better liquidity through the use of leverage. Sivamani Spinning also had positive EBITDs in the post-takeover period. It had a ratio of 7.43 times in the year Y_2, and declined to 5.90 times in the year Y_3.

On the whole, there were two companies with a declining trend in the ratio, four companies with a mixed trend and the remaining two companies with negative EBITDs even in the post-takeover period.

Categorising the companies into those having liquidity and those not having liquidity, by the standard of 8 times (as advocated by James C. Van Horne), the following five units would come under the first category, since the ratio of total debt and equity to EBITD was less than 8 times:

1. Dempo Dairy
2. ICML
3. Bokiyu Tanneries
4. Mico Farm Chemicals
5. Sivamani Spinning

As regards, the shifts in the position prevailing before and after the takeover, the following conclusions emerge:

i. Of the eight units selected for the study, five units had a ratio of less than 8 times, in at least one year after the takeover.

ii. Of the five units which had a ratio of less than 8 times, one unit had a ratio of less than 8 for 4 years after the takeover, another unit had for three years, another for two years and the remaining two for one year each.

iii. The remaining three units out of the sample of eight, not even a single unit had a ratio of less than 8 in any year even after the takeover.

6. IMPACT OF LEVERAGE ON PROFITABILITY

In this section, an attempt had been made to study the impact of leverage on profitability of the sample units. For this purpose the following ratios had been used:

a. Interest Coverage Ratio

b. Interest as a percentage of Total Income

c. Interest as a percentage of Gross Profit

6.1. Interest Coverage Ratio

Interest coverage ratio was one of the most traditional ratios among the leverage ratios. It was a simple ratio of EBIT to the interest charges. This ratio was used to test the firm's debt-servicing capacity. A higher ratio was desirable; but too high a ratio indicates that the firm was very conservative in using debt. A lower ratio indicates excessive use of debt, or inefficient operations.

In the present study, all the sample companies were sick and were in the process of turnaround. As such, the operations would have been inefficient in the pre-takeover period. Their position after takeover needs to be analysed to know whether there was any turnaround or not. There were only negative EBITs in the pre-takeover period as can be seen from the Table–3.9 and some positive EBITs after the takeover. Hence, it was possible to calculate the interest coverage ratios only where EBIT was positive.

Let us, now see how this ratio had changed in the selected sample companies over the study period:

Three companies, Amar Dye-Chem, Bokiyu Tanneries and Coramandal Pharma, had only negative EBITs in all years of the study period.

Dempo Dairy had a positive EBIT in all the years except in Y_{-3} and Y_{-2}. Though this ratio was less than 1 time till year Y_1, it had crossed 1 time in the year Y_2 and reached to the level of 2.2 times in the year Y_3. This had happened because of lower amounts of interest charges against an increasing EBIT.

ICML had an interest coverage ratio of 0.35 times in the year Y_1. However, in the year Y_2 it had become 2.57 times and continued at a level of more than 2 times subsequently. This sudden increase in this ratio was mainly due to a nine-fold increase in EBIT from Rs. 25.46 lakh to Rs. 240.78 lakhs against a marginal increase in interest charges. In the subsequent years, there had been a decline in the interest charges as well as in the EBIT. Amar Dye-Chem had a positive EBIT in only one year before the takeover. Bokiyu Tanneries had a positive EBIT in

Table - 3.9: Interest Coverage Ratio of Sample Units

(Times)

Companies \ Years	Y_{-4}	Y_{-3}	Y_{-2}	Y_{-1}	Y_0	Y_1	Y_2	Y_3	Y_4	Y_5	Y_6
Dempo Dairy	0.93	+	+	0.04	0.70	0.42	1.27	2.20	NA	x	x
ICML	NA	NA	NA	NA	+	0.35	2.57	2.95	2.40	x	x
Amar Dye-Chem	+	+	0.02	+	+	+	+	x	x	x	x
Bokiyu Tanneries	+	+	+	+	+	+	+	+	0.79	+	x
India Precision	+	+	+	+	0.13	0.73	1.31	0.74	1.57	1.31	1.53
Coromandal Pharma	NA	NA	NA	+	+	+	+	+	+	x	x
Mico Farm Chemicals	NA	NA	NA	+	+	1.01	0.56	0.02	2.02	2.55	x
Sivamani Spinning	NA	NA	NA	NA	NA	NA	0.62	2.14	0.61	NA	x

Notes: '+' indicates years where the EBITD is negative.
'NA' indicates data not available.
'x' indicates years beyond year Y_n.

the year Y_4 only. India Precision Bearings had positive EBITs from the year Y_0 onwards. The interest coverage ratio of this company was more than one in a majority of the years, in spite of fluctuations from year to year. One interesting observation is that the interest coverage ratio had decreased in the year Y_3 by almost 50 per cent to 0.74 times from 1.31 times of the previous year Y_2 and again it had increased by more than a hundred per cent in the very next year. Coromandal Pharma never had a positive EBIT during the entire study period. Mico Farm Chemicals had all positive EBITs from the year Y_1 onwards. The interest coverage ratio was about one in the year Y_1. However, it had become 0.56 times in the year Y_2, 0.02 times in the year Y_3 and 2.02 times in the year Y_4. The increasing trend of Y_4 had continued and reached to 2.55 times by the year Y_5.

Sivamani Spinning had positive EBIT in the years Y_2, Y_3 and Y_4. The company had an interest coverage ratio of about 0.60 times in the years Y_2 and Y_4 and a ratio of 2.14 times in the year Y_3.

To summarise, five out of eight sample units had positive EBITs in the post-takeover period for many years and thus they could be said to have turned around on this account. These units are:

1. Dempo Dairy
2. ICML
3. India Precision Bearings
4. Mico Farm Chemicals
5. Sivamani Spinning

6.2. Interest as a percentage of Total Income

This ratio reveals the proportion of interest to total income and how it had changed over time during the study period. The higher the proportion, the greater the burden on the company's profits. A higher proportion of interest may occur owing to the presence of higher debt in the capital structure of the firm, or higher rate of interest or low total Income generated. Under normal conditions, total Income should increase, when the funds are borrowed and put into the business. Higher amount of interest should be followed by higher total income and thereby maintain this ratio at reasonable levels.

In the present study this proportion had varied from a high of 654.31 per cent to a low of 2.04 per cent as can be seen from Table – 3.10.

Let us, now, see how this proportion had been changing over the study period in each of the sample companies.

Dempo Dairy had a ratio of less than 10 per cent before the takeover. It had increased to 12.77 per cent in the year Y_0 and further increased to 31.39 per cent in the year Y_1 and subsequently showed a declining trend. The reason for the sharp increase in this proportion, in the year Y_1, was due to a sudden fall in the total income. Interestingly, the total income had been on a declining trend till the year Y_1, and started increasing from year Y_2.

ICML had a very insignificant income in the year Y_0, as there were no sales. However, it had a proportion of 7.98 per cent by the very next year, Y_1. In the subsequent years the proportion had kept on declining and reached to a low of 2.04 per cent. This declining trend was due to increases in the total income against the moderate changes in the interest burden.

Interest proportion to total income had been increasing from year Y_{-4} to Y_{-1} in case of Amar Dye-Chem. However, it had suddenly declined from 10.81 per cent to 5.35 per cent from year Y_{-1} to Y_0. In the subsequent years it had been about 9 per cent. The reason for this sudden decline in the year Y_0 was due to both a decline in interest amount and an increase in the total income.

Bokiyu Tanneries had a higher proportion of more than 20 per cent in the pre-takeover period. However, it had steadily declined to reach 3.32 per cent by the year Y_4. The reason for the higher proportions before the takeover was due to lower total incomes during that period.

Table - 3.10: Interest as a percentage of Total Income of Sample Units

(In percentages)

Companies / *Years*	Y_{-4}	Y_{-3}	Y_{-2}	Y_{-1}	Y_0	Y_1	Y_2	Y_3	Y_4	Y_5	Y_6
Dempo Dairy	6.94	5.64	11.41	8.57	12.77	31.39	12.45	7.96	NA	x	x
ICML	NA	NA	NA	NA	+	7.98	6.74	3.01	2.04	x	x
Amar Dye-Chem	7.26	7.52	7.85	10.81	5.35	9.14	9.01	x	x	x	x
Bokiyu Tanneries	25.78	42.77	23.21	23.59	14.75	12.98	12.45	7.41	3.32	5.44	x
India Precision	196.43	94.70	59.93	76.11	45.56	19.22	19.10	22.69	16.13	11.54	7.64
Coromandal Pharma	NA	NA	NA	654.31	455.36	158.28	23.61	132.76	217.37	x	x
Mico Farm Chemicals	NA	NA	NA	+	10.78	9.70	8.87	8.81	5.19	6.23	x
Sivamani Spinning	NA	NA	NA	NA	NA	NA	4.98	3.64	4.73	NA	x

Notes: '+' indicates insignificant Total Income, since there was insignificant or no sales.
'NA' indicates data not available.
'x' indicates years beyond year Y_n.

India Precision Bearings had an alarming proportion of about 200 per cent in the year Y_{-4}. However, it had declined steadily from year to year and reached a low of 7.64 per cent. The decline was continuous except in the year Y_3, where there was an increase. The reason for this alarming proportion was that the interest was very high in the year Y_{-4}. However, in the subsequent years the total income had increased continuously at greater pace and the interest had remained at more or less similar levels.

Coromandal Pharma was a strange case among the sample. In this case, the proportion of interest to total income was always much more than a hundred per cent, except in the year Y_2. This implies that the company could not generate more income than the interest.

Mico Farm Chemicals had reasonable proportions of interest to total income after the takeover. It had been less than 10 per cent and had kept on declining over the years in the post-takeover period. In the year Y_5, the proportion had marginally increased to 6.23 per cent from the previous year's 5.19 per cent. The reason for this general declining trend was a steady increase of total income at higher rates and stable interest charges. Sivamani Spinning also had a good proportion of interest to total income at less than 5 per cent for the three years for which data was available.

From the above discussion, it may be concluded that except Coromandal Pharma, all other companies had a declining proportions of interest to total income in the post-takeover period. On the whole, the proportion was at 20 per cent in the post-takeover period. It was only in case of Coromandal Pharma the proportion was very high and the interest was much more than the income generated.

6.3. Interest as a percentage of Gross Profit

This ratio was an attempt to relate the interest with the gross profit. In other words, this ratio attempts to study the firm's ability to meet the first and immediate interest obligations after meeting the cost of goods sold. Therefore, this ratio was a refined measure of knowing the impact of debt on the profitability.

The guiding principle in this ratio is that, if the ratio is more than a hundred per cent, the firm cannot be considered healthy in terms of profitability. It may be noted that in the context of the present study, the gross profit does not include non-operating income.

In the present study, the gross profit was available for only five out of eight units even after the takeover as is evident from Table – 3.11. The remaining three units had continued to suffer gross losses.

Let us now analyse how this ratio had moved over a period of time in these five companies.

Dempo Dairy had exactly hundred percent of this ratio in the year Y_1. In the subsequent years, the ratio has showed a declining trend. There was gross profit during some of the years of the pre-takeover period, but it was highly fluctuating without showing any trend. The company has been earning much more gross profits than the interest burden after the takeover which is a sign of turnaround.

ICML had gross profits only from the year Y_1. In the year Y_1, the ratio was very high at 226.54 per cent and in the subsequent years, it was less than 40 per cent. There was a sharp drop in this ratio from 226.54 per cent to 37.41 per cent in the year Y_2. India Precision also had net losses till the year of takeover. However, after the takeover there had been gross profits. Consequently, this ratio had been calculated from the year Y_0. In this year, the ratio was as high as 277.40 per cent. However, in the subsequent years, this ratio was always less than a hundred per cent. Mico Farm Chemicals also had gross profit from year Y_1, therefore this ratio also had been calculated from the very same year. This ratio had always been less than 50 per cent in the post-takeover period except in the years Y_2 and Y_3.

In the year Y_2 the ratio was 148.11 per cent and in the year Y_3 it was 480.90 per cent. The reason for these extremities was

Table - 3.11: Interest as a Percentage of Gross Profit of Sample Units

(in percentages)

Companies \ Years	Y_{-4}	Y_{-3}	Y_{-2}	Y_{-1}	Y_0	Y_1	Y_2	Y_3	Y_4	Y_5	Y_6
Dempo Dairy	77.58	287.14	+	158.38	89.83	100.00	51.72	37.29	NA	x	x
ICML	NA	NA	NA	NA	+	226.54	37.41	32.55	39.18	x	x
Amar Dye-Chem	+	+	485.89	+	+	+	+	x	x	x	x
Bokiyu Tanneries	+	+	+	+	+	+	+	+	95.91	+	x
India Precision	+	+	+	+	277.40	69.97	55.52	81.48	46.49	52.08	44.40
Coromandal Pharma	NA	NA	NA	+	+	+	+	+	+	x	x
Mico Farm Chemicals	NA	NA	NA	+	+	45.08	148.11	480.90	44.88	36.72	x
Sivamani Spinning	NA	NA	NA	NA	NA	NA	39.39	27.10	64.20	NA	x

Notes: '+' indicates no gross profit in that year.
'NA' indicates data not available.
'x' indicates years beyond year Y_n.

lower gross profit secured by the company. Sivamani Spinning had a ratio of less than a hundred per cent in the years Y_2, Y_3 and Y_4.

On the whole, except Dempo Dairy, all the remaining four units had a mixed trend in this ratio with frequent increases and decreases. However, in the case of Dempo Dairy, the ratio had been declining from the year Y_1 onwards.

From the leverage point of view, interest had proved to be still a dominant component in the structure of expenditure of the companies, emphasising the necessity to take care of the interest burden. As it appears, interest ***per se*** was not posing a problem than the inconsistent operations of the firms. Thus, the sample units were required to concentrate more on the stability of the operations.

7. PATTERN OF FINANCING OF TOTAL ASSETS

In this section, it is proposed to study how the total assets are financed and to what extent these assets are financed from individual sources. In a healthy firm, normally, total assets are financed from equity, total debt and reserves and surpluses, if any. Ideally, total assets and the total of these three financing sources should be equal, if the accounting identity (i.e., assets are equal to capital and liabilities) holds good. But in case of a sick company, there would not be any reserves and surpluses and there would be accumulated losses. As a result of this, total assets would be less than the total amount of equity and debt. This happens because of the reason that a portion of these two financing sources would be appropriated by the losses accumulated over the years. As the firm turns around, these losses would gradually be reduced. If every thing goes well, the proportion of financing through equity and debt should increase and match the total of assets.

In the context of what was described above, let us analyse the pattern of financing of each of the sample companies in detail. As the sample units are sick companies, there were no reserves and surpluses and only accumulated losses were present. In order to comprehend the changes in the financing pattern of the selected units, a comparison was made between the figures of Y_o (the year of takeover) and Y_n (the latest year of takeover for which data are available).

7.1. Dempo Dairy

In case of Dempo Dairy, a comparison of financing pattern of total assets has been done between the years Y_o and Y_3, as shown in Table – 3.12. The equity capital has not changed during this period and remained at the same level. However, the total assets have increased by about 50 per cent of the assets of year Y_o by the year Y_n. There has been an increase in the current liabilities but a good decrease in the long-term liabilities. As a result of the huge decrease in the long-term liabilities, the accumulated losses also declined by more than 50 per cent. On the whole it may be concluded that the declining accumulated losses balance and increasing total assets indicate that the firm is turning around after the takeover.

Table - 3.12 : Pattern of Financing Total Assets of Dempo Dairy

Years / *Items*	Y_o		Y_3	
	(Rs. in lakh)	*(% ages)*	*(Rs. in lakh)*	*(% ages)*
Current Liabilities	66.00	24.54	94.00	23.80
Long-term Liabilities	723.00	268.77	464.00	117.47
Equity	95.00	35.32	95.00	24.05
Reserves & Surpluses (Accumulated P&L A/C)	-615.00	-228.63	-258.00	-65.32
Total Assets	269.00	100.00	395.00	100.00

7.2 ICML

In case of ICML, a comparison of financing pattern of total assets has been done to years Y_o and Y_4 as is evident from Table–3.13. The amount of equity capital has not changed between these two years. However, the total assets were so low that they were about 80 per cent of the equity in the year Y_0 whereas the total assets had increased substantially to bring down the same to the level of about 40 per cent of total assets. Similarly, with regard to debt, the total assets were so low that the total debt was more than 567 per cent of total assets in the year Y_0 and it has improved to about 134 per cent by the year Y_4. In absolute figures, the debt has increased from Rs. 683.80 lakh to Rs. 1,006.81 lakh from the year Y_0 to Y_4. But the total assets have increased from Rs. 120.50 lakh to Rs. 750.67 lakh in the same period. This multi-fold increase in assets against a little increase of debt has brought down the accumulated losses from the year Y_0 to Y_4. This signifies, the operation of 'trading on equity'. This can be considered as a character of turnaround after the takeover.

Table - 3.13 : Pattern of Financing Total Assets of ICML

Years / *Items*	Y_0		Y_4	
	(Rs. in lakh)	*(% ages)*	*(Rs. in lakh)*	*(% ages)*
Current Liabilities	210.63	174.80	297.51	39.63
Long-term Liabilities	473.17	392.67	709.30	94.49
Equity	303.95	79.78	303.95	40.49
Reserves & Surpluses (Accumulated P&L A/C)	-867.25	-547.25	-560.09	-74.61
Total Assets	120.50	100.00	750.67	100.00

7.3. Amar Dye-Chem

Amar Dye-Chem has only two years of history after the takeover, therefore, a comparison is made in Table – 3.14 between the takeover year (Y_0) and the latest year after takeover, that is year Y_2. In this case also, there was no significant change in the amount of equity. However, the total assets had decreased from Rs. 5,017.72 lakh to Rs. 3,883.14 lakh from year Y_0 to Y_2.

This obviously has increased the equity to total assets proportion from Rs. 4,944.89 lakh to Rs. 5,858.41 lakh from year Y_0 to Y_2.

Interestingly, there have been contrasting changes in short-term liabilities and long-term liabilities. The short-term liabilities have increased tremendously, whereas the long-term liabilities declined drastically. Besides these, the accumulated loss also has doubled. In spite of all this, the total assets have come down. Therefore, it may be concluded that the company has not used the increased debt amount to create assets and also increased the accumulated losses. Hence, it may be concluded that the company had not showed any sign of improvement or turnaround.

Table - 3.14 : Pattern of Financing Total Assets of Amar Dye-Chem

Years	Y_0		Y_2	
Items	*(Rs. in lakh)*	*(% ages)*	*(Rs. in lakh)*	*(% ages)*
Current Liabilities	3,956.63	78.85	5,646.27	145.40
Long-term Liabilities	988.26	19.70	212.14	5.46
Equity Reserves & Surpluses	2,233.69	44.52	2,233.79	57.63
(Accumulated P&L A/C)	-2,160.86	-43.07	-4,209.06	-108.39
Total Assets	5,017.72	100.00	3,883.14	100.00

7.4. Bokiyu Tanneries

In case of Bokiyu Tanneries, the comparison is made between Y_0 and Y_5 in Table – 3.15. There has been no change in the equity capital in these years. However, the total assets have increased from Rs. 91.26 lakh to Rs. 2,260.81 lakh from the year Y_0 to Y_5. This is an increase of about 25 times. The total debt also is about 225 per cent of the total assets in the year Y_0 and is brought down to about 75 per cent. In absolute figures, both the total debt and total assets have increased. The total debt has increased by less than 5 times, in comparison to 25 times increase in total assets. This implies that the company has created more assets than the increase in debt and thereby eliminates accumulated loss completely. The increase in debt is more in the form of short-term debt. On the whole, the company has made a smart recovery and turned around with higher proportions of debt. This can also be seen from the fact that in the year Y_0 there are accumulated losses over and above the reserves and surpluses portion and the situation has turned around completely by the year Y_5. There is a positive balance of reserves and surpluses after wiping out all the accumulated losses and these reserves and surpluses contributed about 15 per cent of the total assets.

Table - 3.15 : Pattern of Financing Total Assets of Bokiyu Tanneries

Years / *Items*	Y_0		Y_5	
	(Rs.in lakh)	*(% ages)*	*(Rs.in lakh)*	*(% ages)*
Current Liabilities	205.91	225.63	1691.97	74.84
Long-term Liabilities	192.45	210.88	179.06	7.92
Equity	49.91	54.69	49.91	2.21
Reserves & Surpluses (Accumulated P&L A/C)	-357.01	-391.20	339.87	15.0 3
Total Assets	91.26	100.00	2,260.81	100.00

7.5. India Precision Bearings

In case of India Precision Bearings, the comparison is between years Y_0 and Y_6 as shown in Table – 3.16. In this case also there are no significant changes in the equity. However, its proportion to total assets has changed from Y_0 to Y_6. It was about 30 per cent in the year Y_0 but came down to about 19 per cent by the year Y_6. Obviously, this was due to an increase in the total assets. The total assets have increased from Rs. 971.18 lakh to Rs. 1,581.18 lakh from year Y_0 to Y_6, an increase of over 60 per cent.

The total debt has also increased from Rs. 1,642.22 lakh to Rs. 1,854.66 lakh during the period Y_0 to Y_6. This is an increase of just 13 per cent in comparison to the increase of 60 per cent in the total assets. This greater rate of increase has reduced the accumulated losses of year Y_0 from Rs. 970.96 lakh to Rs. 573.48 lakh by the year Y_6. This change is an indication of turnaround. The accumulated loss has been brought down to 36.27 per cent from 99.97 per cent from the year Y_0 to Y_6.

Table - 3.16 : Pattern of Financing Total Assets of India Precision Bearings

Years / *Items*	Y_0		Y_6	
	(Rs.in lakh)	*(% ages)*	*(Rs.in lakh)*	*(% ages)*
Current Liabilities	325.65	33.53	308.42	19.51
Long-term Liabilities	1,316.57	135.56	1,546.24	97.79
Equity Reserves & Surpluses	299.92	30.88	300.00	18.97
(Accumulated P&L A/C)	-970.96	-99.97	-573.48	-36.27
Total Assets	971.18	100.00	1,581.18	100.00

7.6. Coromandal Pharma

In case of Coromandal Pharma, a comparison is made between the year Y_0 and Y_4 (Table – 3.17) in order to study the changes in financing pattern of total assets. The equity has increased by more than 10 times from the year Y_0 to Y_4 from Rs. 43.98 lakh to Rs. 512.87 lakh. Also the total debt has increased from Rs. 416.39 lakh to Rs. 802.31 lakh. An increase of little less than a hundred per cent. However, the total assets have increased by over 4 times from year Y_0 from Rs. 107.30 lakh to Rs. 586.84 lakh for year Y_4. The accumulated losses have also doubled from Rs. 353.07 lakh in the year Y_0 to Rs. 728.34 lakh in the year Y_4. All these increases reveal the fact that the increases in total debt and equity put together are not reflected fully in the increase of total assets because of the reason that the increase of Rs. 375.27 lakh in the accumulated losses is compensated by the increase in equity and total debt.

Table - 3.17 : Pattern of Financing Total Assets of Coromandal Pharma

Years / *Items*	Y_0		Y_4	
	(Rs.in lakh)	*(% ages)*	*(Rs.in lakh)*	*(% ages)*
Current Liabilities	113.23	105.53	196.82	33.54
Long-term Liabilities	303.16	282.53	605.49	103.18
Equity	43.98	40.99	512.87	87.40
Reserves & Surpluses (Accumulated P&L A/C)	-353.07	-329.05	-728.34	-124.12
Total Assets	107.30	100.00	586.84	100.00

7.7. Mico Farm Chemicals

Mico Farm Chemicals has five years of post-takeover data and, hence, a comparison is made between years Y_0 and Y_5 in Table – 3.18. The equity of this company has increased by a little less than 50 per cent from Rs. 67.50 lakh to Rs. 94.50 lakh. The total debt has also increased by about 1.5 times from Rs. 437.87 lakh to Rs. 1,089.37 lakh. The total assets have increased by almost 3 times and the accumulated losses of Rs. 196.79 lakh in the year Y_0 are completely wiped out and positive reserves and surpluses of Rs. 13.06 lakh are noted by the year Y_5. This is an evidence of turnaround of the company.

Table - 3.18 : Pattern of Financing Total Assets of Mico Farm Chemicals

Years / Items	Y_0		Y_5	
	(Rs. in lakh)	*(% ages)*	*(Rs. in lakh)*	*(% ages)*
Current Liabilities	58.54	18.97	695.88	58.14
Long-term Liabilities	379.33	122.93	393.49	32.87
Equity	67.50	21.87	94.50	7.90
Reserves & Surpluses (Accumulated P&L A/C)	-196.79	-63.77	13.06	1.09
Total Assets	308.58	100.00	1,196.93	100.00

7.8 Sivamani Spinning

In Table – 3.19, a comparison is made in case of Sivamani Spinning between year Y_{-2} and Y_4 since the data is not available for all the years. The equity has increased by about 35 per cent from Rs. 72.20 lakh to Rs. 100.00 lakh during the above period.

Table - 3.19: Pattern of Financing Total Assets of Sivamani Spinning

Years / Items	Y_{-2}		Y_4	
	(Rs. in lakh)	*(% ages)*	*(Rs. in lakh)*	*(% ages)*
Current Liabilities	67.35	27.85	307.64	89.10
Long-term Liabilities	216.76	89.65	124.02	35.92
Equity	72.20	29.86	100.00	28.96
Reserves & Surpluses (Accumulated P&L A/C)	-114.52	-47.36	-186.38	-53.98
Total Assets	241.79	100.00	345.28	100.00

The total debt has also increased by about 50 per cent from Rs. 284.11 lakh to Rs. 431.66 lakh during the same period. The total assets have increased by about 40 per cent. The accumulated losses have also increased by about 60 per cent from Rs. 114.52 lakh to Rs. 186.38 lakh by the year Y_4. Since, the amount of accumulated losses have increased, it may be concluded that the increase in total debt and equity put together is more than the increase in total assets and the accumulated losses have used up a portion of the increase in total debt and equity to the extent of Rs. 71.86 lakh. It may be concluded that even after the takeover the sources of finance are being appropriated for losses. This shows that the company has not turned around even after the takeover.

It is evident from the above discussion that five out of eight sample units are able to register improvement after the takeover. Among the five, two companies namely, Bokiyu Tanneries and Mico Farm Chemicals had been able to wipe out all their accumulated losses and left some surplus also. Whereas, the other three companies, viz., Dempo Dairy, ICML, India Precision could reduce their losses and improve their assets. The remaining three units, Amar Dye-Chem, Coromandal Pharma and Sivamani Spinning, have increased their accumulated losses even after the takeover and used up those funds, which would have otherwise been used for the financing of a portion of the total assets. Therefore, these three are the companies that could not turnaround even after the takeover.

8. FINDINGS

An attempt has been made in this chapter to study the leverage of the sample units in terms of the trends and its impact, with particular reference to the improvement or otherwise, recorded by the units taken-up for the study. Such an attempt has led us to the following conclusions:

1. When an attempt was made to measure the leverage through usual techniques it was found to be erroneous and unreliable, as the figures used for such an exercise had turned out to be negative for a majority of the years in the sample

units. As such, the study depended on the analysis of leverage through certain ratios suggested in the finance literature.

2. Studied thus, the debt-equity ratio, one of the important indicators of leverage, had increased in the very first year of takeover (Y_1) in the following units. That was to say, the equity of these companies was more or less static and the debt finance had been used for the needs of turnaround:

1. Dempo Dairy
2. Bokiyu Tanneries
3. India Precision Bearings, and
4. Mico Farm Chemicals

3. The following companies enhanced the equity for the purpose of implementing turnaround after the takeover:

1. ICML
2. Amar Dye-Chem
3. Coromandal Pharma
4. Sivamani Spinning

4. The study reveals the fact that in most of the sample units, total debt was in excess of the total assets even after the takeover. Consequently, the creditors are at a greater risk, as the assets are not sufficient to meet their loan obligations. Though, there has been a general decline in the proportion of total debt to total assets in most of the sample units, only three companies, viz. Bokiyu Tanneries, Coromandal Pharma and Mico Farm Chemicals, have a ratio of less than one time in the year Y_n. This implies that the creditors in these three companies are secure as the total assets are in excess of the total debt.

5. In the present study, most of the companies have low equity compared to total assets. Equity capital as a percentage of total assets was varying between the lowest of 2 per cent and the highest of 87 per cent. Further there was a declining trend in the proportion of equity to total assets among the sample units.

6. Normally, in a healthy unit, the total assets are financed by the equity, debt and retained earnings. Therefore, the total of assets would always be more than the total of equity and debt put together. In this study, the total assets were always less than a hundred per cent in the pre-takeover period. However, the situation has gradually improved over the post-takeover period in a majority of the units. Hence, it can be concluded that the accumulated losses have gradually declined and there are reserves and surpluses in some cases, thus implying turnaround after the takeover.

7. The ratio of EBITD to total debt has been positive in most of the sample units after the takeover. Out of the eight units selected for the study there were two units, which have an ever -increasing ratio, four companies have a mixed trend with frequent increases and decreases and the remaining two companies have no positive ratio. This indicates that only the last two units have failed to turnaround even with the change in management from the point of view of liquidity.

8. The ratio of Total Debt and Equity to Earnings Before Interest Taxes and Depreciation reveal the extent of earnings available to cover the debt and equity obligations at a given point of time. Usually, a ratio of more than 8 times is said to be an alarming level. In the present analysis as many as five units have a ratio of less than 8 times in at least one of the years after the takeover. Thus implying that these units have turned around and the proportion of earnings have improved thereby resulting in decline in this ratio. The remaining 3 units never had a ratio of less than 8 times even after the takeover.

9. Since, all units selected for study were sick units and are in the process of turnaround, the EBIT of these units would have naturally been negative before the takeover and in case of some it would have become positive after the takeover. Therefore, it was possible to calculate the interest coverage ratios of only these companies. In this category, there were only five companies out of the eight samples selected for the study. Since, there have been better interest coverage ratios in these

companies after the takeover, it may be concluded that these companies have turned around.

10. Since the proportion of interest to EBIT had not revealed many insights, it was decided to compare the interest charges with the total income. As a general rule, the interest burden increases when the debt burden increases and when the debt increases it should normally go into productive use and should help in increasing the total income. This need not be always true in the case of sick units. It is found that all the sample units (except Coromandal Pharma) have declining proportions of interest to total income after the takeover. Normally, this kind of decline occurs in three situations as is evident from the analysis: (a) A decreasing interest burden with stable total income or (b) An increasing total income with stable interest charges or (c) Both a decrease in the interest burden and an increase in the total income. Because of one of the above reasons the proportion has been declining after the takeover.

11. Interest as a percentage of gross profits reveals the ability of the firm to meet the interest obligations. In the present study, it is found that five out of eight units have gross profits in the post-takeover period. This ratio shows a mixed trend in four out of these five units; even in the post-takeover period and the remaining one unit is continuously declining. However, all these five units have positive gross profit figures. Thus, these units are considered to be units where the efforts of turnaround have worked well.

12. On analysing the pattern of financing the assets of these sample units, it was found that five of the eight units could reduce their accumulated losses and were able to register improvement after the takeover. Among these five units, two units were able to wipe out their accumulated losses completely and register surpluses. The remaining three of the sample eight units had increased their accumulated losses even after the takeover. These three units had used up a portion of funds that would have normally been used for financing assets.

REFERENCES

1. Hampton, J. John (1986), *Financial Decision Making: Concepts, Problems and Cases*, Prentice - Hall of India Private Ltd., New Delhi, and p. 194.
2. Khan, M.Y., and Jain, P.K. (1992), *Financial Management: Text and Problems*, Tata McGraw Hill Publishing Company Ltd., New Delhi, p. 417.
3. Joy, O.M. (1977), *Introduction to Financial Management* (Homewood Ill.) Irwin, and p. 226.
4. Gitman, L.J. (1976), *Principles of Management Finance*, Harper & Row, New York, p. 84.
5. Agarwal, N.P. (1981), *Analysis of Financial Statements: A Case Study of Aluminium Industry in India*, National Publishing House, New Delhi.
6. Batty, J. (1980), *Accountancy for Managers*, Allied Publishers, Delhi.
7. Prasad, G., and Rao, K.V. (1989), *Financial Management in Public Sector Enterprises*, Ashish Publishing House, New Delhi, Chapter - 7.
8. Lawrence D. Schall and Charles W. Haley (1986), *Introduction to Financial Management*, McGraw Hill Book Company, Singapore.
9. *ICICI Portfolio* (1993-94) Published by ICICI Ltd., Bombay.
10. Prasad, G., and Rao, K.V. (1989), *op. cit.*
11. Van Horne, James. C. (1995), *Financial Management and Policy*, Prentice-Hall of India Pvt. Ltd., New Delhi, pp. 770-71.
12. Prasad, G., and Rao, K.V. (1989), *op. cit.*

Chapter IV

PROFITABILITY ANALYSIS

In this chapter an attempt has been made to study the profitability analysis of the sample units. In addition to this, in Part - II, an attempt has also been made to verify whether the better-known managements are able to turnaround the units faster and whether the firms are expanding after the takeover.

PART - I

Part - I of this chapter is to study the effect of the takeover in turning the company around through the profitability performance. A comparison of the profit performance of the sample units is made between the pre- and the post-takeover periods. For this purpose the following hypothesis has been set.

1. HYPOTHESIS

When a company has been taken over by the new management, the company should turnaround and the profitability should improve.

2. INTRODUCTION

The ultimate test of any business enterprise is profit. Perhaps the most important reason for keeping accounts is that the information contained in them provides the means of measuring the progress of the business or 'testing its pulse'; and of indicating when and where remedial action, if necessary, shall be taken.[1] These days managements are giving top priority to increase the profits and maximise their shareholders' wealth. The efficiency of a management is measured in terms of profit generated by the business. It is sometimes said that higher profitability implies greater efficiency.[2]

The word 'profitability' may be defined as the ability of a given investment to earn a return from its use.[3] The profitability of a firm has a direct bearing on its growth. This is principally due to the psychological incentives and the financial resources that the profitability provides. High profitability makes it possible to plough back substantial resources; helps raise equity capital and loans in the capital market.

Apart from the owners, the management of the company, and the creditors, both long-term and short-term, could be interested in the financial soundness of the firm. The management of a firm is, generally, eager to measure its operating efficiency in terms of profits. Similarly, owners invest their funds with an expectation of a reasonable return. The operating efficiency of a firm and its ability to ensure adequate return to its shareholders depends ultimately on the profits earned. Moreover, profits provide money for repaying the debt used to finance the project and the resources for expansion.

3. MESUREMENT OF PROFITABILITY

Profitability of a firm can be measured by its profitability ratios. In this section it is attempted to study the various ratios suggested for measuring the performance in relation to profitability.

N.P. Agarwal[4] has analyzed the profitability in Aluminum Industry using the following ratios:

1. Return on Capital Employed
2. Return on Long-term Investment
3. Cost of Long-term Borrowings
4. Return on Equity Shareholders' Funds
5. Rate of Dividend Paid on Equity Share Capital

John J. Hampton[5] has suggested two major categories of profitability ratios: (i) Profits in relation to Sales and (ii) Profits in relation to Assets. The ratios suggested by him are:

1. Profit Margin
2. Gross Profit Margin
3. Asset Turnover
4. Return on Investment
5. Return on Equity
6. Earnings Power
7. Times Interest Earned

Lawrence D. Schall and Charles W. Haley[6] have suggested the following for analysing the profitability of a company:

1. Gross Profit Margin
2. Net Operating Margin
3. Profit Margin on Sales
4. Return on Total Assets
5. Return on Equity

James C. Van Horne[7] also has suggested the following profitability ratio in relation to Sales and in relation to Investment.

I. Profitability in relation to Sales
   1. Gross Profit Margin
   2. Net Profit Margin

II. Profitability in relation to Investments
   3. Rate of return on Equity
   4. Return on Asset Ratio
   5. Net Operating Profit rate of return

Industrial Credit and Investment Corporation of India (ICICI), a leading Development Financial Institution publishes annually a detailed study[8] on various aspects of the aggregate financial performance of its assisted units. In these studies profitability has been studied through the following ratios:

1. Gross Profit as a percentage of Sales
2. Gross Profit as a percentage of Total Net Assets
3. Return on Capital Employed
4. Profits Before Tax as a percentage of Sales
5. Profits Before Tax as a percentage of Net worth
6. Profits After Tax as a percentage of Net worth
7. Retained Profits as a percentage of profits After Tax
8. Operating Cash flow as a percentage of Gross Capital
9. Operating Cash flow as a percentage of Sales

The Reserve Bank of India (RBI) also compiles on a regular basis, statistics pertaining to the growth and working of joint stock companies in India.[9] For this purpose the RBI uses some selected Financial and other Ratios, which include profitability and profit allocation ratios. These are:

1. Gross Profits to Total Net Assets
2. Gross Profits to Sales
3. Profit After Tax to Net worth
4. Tax Provision to Profits Before Tax
5. Profits Retained to Profit After Tax
6. Dividends to Net worth.
7. Current Dividends to total Paid-up Capital.

After considering the above, the following ratios appear to be most commonly used:

1. Gross Profit Margin $= \frac{\text{Gross Profit}}{\text{Sales}} \times 100$

2. Gross Profit as a percentage of Total Net Assets

$$= \frac{\text{Gross Profit}}{\text{Total Net Assets}} \times 100$$

3. Net Profit Margin $= \dfrac{\text{EBIT}}{\text{Sales}} \times 100$

4. Return on Assets

$$= \frac{\text{Net Profit after Taxes + Interest}}{\text{Total Assets}} \times 100$$

5. Return on Capital Employed

$$= \frac{\text{Net Profit after Tax}}{\text{Total Capital Employed}} \times 100$$

6. Return on Equity Shareholders' Equity

$$= \frac{\text{Net Income to Common Shareholders}}{\text{Common Stockholders' Equity}} \times 100$$

7. Profit after Tax as percentage of Net worth

$$= \frac{\text{Profit after Tax}}{\text{Net Worth}} \times 100$$

8. Profits Retained to Profits after Tax

$$= \frac{\text{Profits Retained}}{\text{Profits after Tax}} \times 100$$

Though, normally, it is attempted to study the profitability performance with the help of the ratio analysis. In this study an attempt is made to analyze the profitability through the following:

1. Absolute Profit Figures
2. Decomposition of Total Income and Expenditure
3. Proportions and Ratios

In addition to ratio tests, absolute profit figures are analyzed for the reason that the sample units were sick before the takeover and some are being turned around gradually and entered the profits stage, whereas some more are still incurring losses but are turning around with declining losses. The trends of profitability may not be so visible if studied through ratios alone. Hence, the above order has been adopted to see the changes in the profitability position before and after the takeover.

An attempt has been made to study the profit (loss) figures in absolute terms with a specific focus on individual sample units selected for the study in addition to decomposition analysis and proportions and ratios of the items under Income and Expenditure of the sample units.

4. ABSOLUTE ANALYSIS

In this section, an attempt has been made to study the profitability of each of the sample units over the study period with the help of absolute profit figures like Gross Profit, EBIT, Operating Profit and Net Profit. In addition to this, the decomposition analysis of Expenditure and Income also had been done to see the changes over the study period. The data and discussion have been presented company-wise.

4.1. Dempo Dairy

The gross profit of this company was positive for majority of the years of the study period, though it has not been stable before the year of takeover, i.e., Y_0. As can be seen from Table 4.1, there was gross loss of Rs. 88.8 lakhs in the year Y_{-2} and this

Table - 4.1: Different Profit Figures of Sample Units for the Study Period

(Rs. in lakh)

Companies	Profit \ Years	Y_{-4}	Y_{-3}	Y_{-2}	Y_{-1}	Y_0	Y_1	Y_2	Y_3	Y_4	Y_5	Y_6
Dempo Dairy	Gross Profit	98.90	14.31	-88.87	40.75	59.00	43.00	58.00	118.00	NA	x	x
	EBIT	71.38	-8.57	-125.85	2.76	37.00	18.00	38.00	97.00	NA	x	x
	Op. Profit	-5.35	-49.65	-204.13	-61.77	-16.00	-25.00	8.00	53.00	NA	x	x
	Net Profit	2.80	-25.66	-97.49	-54.50	-91.00	-14.00	38.00	93.00	NA	x	x
ICML	Gross Profit	NA	NA	NA	NA	-8.38	32.56	250.18	161.52	106.70	x	x
	EBIT	NA	NA	NA	NA	-13.38	25.46	240.78	155.00	100.28	x	x
	Op. Profit	NA	NA	NA	NA	-100.76	-48.30	147.18	102.42	58.48	x	x
	Net Profit	NA	NA	NA	NA	-99.77	57.43	90.01	84.35	77.86	x	x
Amar Dye-Chem	Gross Profit	-49.87	-94.27	84.62	-1131.83	-495.05	-642.22	-401.70	x	x	x	x
	EBIT	-131.82	-165.24	6.23	-1914.69	-537.23	-688.69	-450.06	x	x	x	x
	Op. Profit	-465.11	-529.98	-404.93	-2441.10	-844.72	-1073.56	-852.36	x	x	x	x
	Profit	25.31	74.91	46.22	-2095.38	651.65	-844.60	-859.36	x	x	x	x
Rokiyu Tanneries	Gross Profit	-41.97	-65.26	-76.93	-169.59	-208.73	-217.53	-103.94	-353.71	67.26	-120.81	x
	EBIT	-49.85	-70.27	-80.35	-173.06	-211.79	-225.21	-126.67	-374.21	50.92	-136.04	x
	Op. Profit	-67.07	-92.29	-98.89	-201.75	-235.53	-261.90	-208.90	-464.91	-13.59	-239.79	x
	Net Profit	-61.41	-43.38	-19.37	-84.23	-77.33	32.53	40.45	98.70	242.53*	31.43*	x
India Precision	Gross Profit	-131.00	-21.63	-30.14	-42.00	68.19	166.86	211.32	151.43	241.90	209.15	222.18
	EBIT	-174.00	-64.73	-73.26	- 74.00	24.8	85.62	153.95	91.54	176.89	142.90	150.53
	Op. Profit	-284.00	-196.13	-227.27	-211.00	-164.35	-31.13	36.62	-31.85	64.44	33.98	51.88
	Net Profit	-219.00	-203.23	-219.73	-139.00	-108.72	10.11	52.34	-26.19	73.45	48.20	70.88

(Contd...)

Companies	Profit \ Years	Y_{-4}	Y_{-3}	Y_{-2}	Y_{-1}	Y_0	Y_1	Y_2	Y_3	Y_4	Y_5	Y_6
Coromandal Pharm	Gross Profit	NA	NA	NA	-9.48	-13.20	-6.10	-18.91	-34.77	-55.13	x	x
	EBIT	NA	NA	NA	-15.75	-19.52	-7.13	-35.94	-52.49	-71.29	x	x
	Op. Profit	NA	NA	NA	-64.30	-71.34	-11.41	-82.91	-121.73	-147.11	x	x
	Net Profit	NA	NA	NA	-57.65	-61.07	-10.44	-57.19	-150.05	-204.5O	x	x
Mico Farm Chemicals	Gross Profit	NA	NA	NA	-19.59	-84.63	144.28	62.02	17.33	190.19	258.93	x
	EBIT	NA	NA	NA	-19.60	-99.61	135.95	51.47	1.98	172.51	242.50	x
	Op. Profit	NA	NA	NA	-78.61	-118.17	70.91	-40.39	-81.36	87.15	147.42	x
	Net Profit	NA	NA	NA	-78.58	-45.53	4.84	1.22	40.59	85.44	163.92*	x
Sivamani Spinning	Gross Profit	NA	NA	NA	NA	NA	NA	51.97	75.49	40.14	NA	x
	EBIT	NA	NA	NA	NA	NA	NA	12.75	43.82	15.63	NA	x
	Op. Profit	NA	NA	NA	NA	NA	NA	-7.72	23.36	-10.14	NA	x
	Net Profit	-13.83	-29.21	-22.45	NA	NA	NA	4.89	27.59	-3.86	NA	x

Notes: '*' There has been provision for tax in these two cases for only three years and there are no other cases of tax provisions in the entire study, hence the tax effect has been ignored.

'+' Figures of Y_1, Y_2 and Y_3 of Cormandal Pharma have been reduced proportionately to 12 months.

'NA' indicates data not available

'X' indicates years beyond year Y_n.

turned out to be a profit of Rs. 118 lakh in year Y_3. To be more precise, in year Y_{-2} the cost of goods sold is 110 per cent of sales. After the takeover, the cost of goods sold had always been less than net sales. The Net Profit Before Interest and Taxes in the Dempo Dairy during the study period had been recorded both positive and negative, variously. EBIT has registered positive amounts after the takeover.

The Operating Profit for the Dempo Dairy had been negative till the year Y_1 and it became positive from the year Y_2. It implies that there had been a turnaround after the takeover in the year Y_2. Another interesting observation from the presented data was that there had been a steady decline in the interest burden of the Dempo Dairy during the study period, which had resulted in improved profits. As there had been no significant profits (mostly net losses) and thereby no Provisions for Taxes, the concepts of profit used in this analysis like Profit Before Tax (PBT) or Profit After Tax (PAT), both mean one and the same. It is evident from the Table – 4.1 that profit before tax was higher than the operating profit (in many cases the net loss was lower than the operating loss). This was because of the presence of significant amounts of non-operating income throughout the study period. The non-operating income was as high as Rs.106.65 lakh in the year Y_2, which was almost 25 per cent of the operating income. This abnormal non-operating income (Rs. 85.29 lakh) mainly had come from milk processing.

Decomposition Analysis: Table - 4.2 presents decomposition of Total Expenditure and Total Income. As one can see from the information contained in the table, there is a set pattern and the trend is quite random.

The data on expenditure pattern in Dempo Dairy has been presented in Table -4.2. The total expenditure had declined in the year Y_1 and thereafter it had continuously increased. Similarly, the material cost also declined in proportion to the expenditure, in the year Y_1 and improved subsequently. The remaining heads of expenditure like wages, interest, depreciation and other expenses had increased manifold in the year Y_1 and started declining from the year Y_2 onwards.

Table - 4.2: Decomposition of Total Expenditure and Income of Dempo Dairy after the takeover

(In percentages)

Items \ Years	Y_0	Y_1	Y_2	Y_3	Y_4
Material	65.01	1.92	25.34	53.83	NA
Employees (Wages)	7.57	25.00	20.81	12.22	NA
Other expenses	9.69	29.49	31.23	20.49	NA
Interest	12.53	27.56	13.57	9.11	NA
Depreciation	5.20	16.03	9.05	4.35	NA
I. Total Expenditure	100.00 (423.00)	100.00 (156.00)	100.00 (221.00)	100.00 (483.00)	NA NA
Operating Income	122.59	92.25	88.42	93.06	NA
Non-operating Income	2.41	4.23	4.63	2.95	NA
Changes in Stock	-24.70	3.52	6.95	3.99	NA
II. Total Income	100.00 (332.00)	100.00 (142.00)	100.00 (259.00)	100.00 (576.00)	NA NA
III. Net Profit/ Loss	(-91.00)	(-14.00)	(38.00)	(93.00)	NA

Note: Figures within parentheses are absolute amounts in lakh of rupees.

Table - 4.2 also shows the way the income has been generated. Though in the year Y_0, there had been a decline of 24.70 per cent in the value of stock, in the subsequent years it had been positive and had contributed between 3 per cent and 7 per cent of the total income. The operating income also had been about 90 per cent and the non-operating income varied between 2 per cent and 5 per cent. This indicated that the major portion of the income had been coming from business operations. The gap between the total expenditure and total income, i.e., net profit turned out to be negative in the years Y_0 and Y_1 and positive from year Y_2. Moreover, even the negative balance of year Y_0 had reduced significantly in the year Y_1 and became positive from year Y_2. This was a clear indication of turnaround after the takeover.

4.2. ICML

Though there are fluctuations in the gross profits from year to year, they have been always positive after the takeover. One general observation at this stage is that the margin between the cost of goods sold and income from net sales is shrinking from the year Y_2 to Y_4. This is a matter of concern and needs serious examination. EBIT also shows a similar trend in the sample period. The depreciation figures are very small and are following the same trend as gross profits and EBIT.

The operating profit has been negative in the years Y_0 and Y_1 and subsequently it has been positive in the years Y_2, Y_3 and Y_4. However, there has been a decline in the operating profits from the year Y_2 to Y_4. The reason for this trend can be found out while doing decomposition analysis.

The profits before tax are also following the same trend as gross profit and operating profits, but the variation from year to year has been narrowed down. This has happened mainly because of the effect of non-operating income. This non-operating income, as indicated earlier, includes adjustment in stocks to a significant level.

Decomposition Analysis: Table – 4.3 shows a picture of the proportions of Total Expenses and Total Income from year to year after the takeover.

Table – 4.3, indicates that the proportion of cost of material has been gradually increasing over the period from Y_1 to Y_4. Cost of Employees and other costs were by and large stable. The interest component in the total cost had been steadily declining. It had reduced by about 50 per cent from year Y_2 to Y_3. Even, the item depreciation also followed the same trend.

Table – 4.3 also presents a picture of total income and its structural distribution. The total income was highly dominated by the operating income, though a significant proportion of the effect of changes in stock also present in it. However, this effect was slowly vanishing.

Table - 4.3: Decomposition of Total Expenditure and Income of ICML after the Takeover

(In Percentages)

Items \ Years	Y_0	Y_1	Y_2	Y_3	Y_4
Material	Nil	72.34	73.57	80.37	81.59
Employees	0.82	8.62	8.32	7.39	8.30
Other Costs	7.50	10.63	9.83	8.63	7.68
Interest	86.72	7.67	7.58	3.21	2.11
Depreciation	4.96	0.74	0.76	0.40	0.32
I. Total Expenditure	100.00 (100.76)	100.00 (964.63)	100.00 (1234.48)	100.00 (1640.20)	100.00 (1984.45)
Operating Income	Nil	89.66	104.32	101.05	99.06
Non-Operating Income	100	0.81	0.56	0.37	0.49
Changes in Stock	Nil	9.53	-4.88	-1.42	0.45
II .Total Income	100.00 (0.99)	100.00 (1022.06)	100.00 (1324.49)	100.00 (1724.55)	100.00 (2062.31)
III. Net Profit/ Loss	(-99.77)	(57.43)	(90.01)	(84.35)	(77.86)

Note: Figures within parentheses are absolute amounts in lakh of rupees.

The difference between total income and total cost is positive and it is about 5 per cent of the total income. Unfortunately, it has been gradually declining. This is because of the ever-increasing material costs. To conclude, even though, the company has turned around in the very first year of its takeover, there has been a declining trend from the year Y_3 onwards.

4.3. Amar Dye-Chem

The Gross Profits of this company had always been negative except in the year Y_{-2}. In the very next year the company suffered a huge gross loss owing to increase in the cost of material, expenditure on personnel and other expenses and a new provision of Rs. 285 lakh for liabilities relating to earlier years for the disputed matters like excise duty, interest on power charges, sales tax, which were pending with various authorities. The depreciation provision was also unusually high at Rs. 783 lakh in that year. Moreover, there had been no consistent trend during the study period. In the first year of the takeover (year Y_0), the gross loss had drastically increased; and in the very next year the loss showed a decline. This decrease could be due to turnaround of the company after takeover.

As far as operating profit is concerned, there had been losses in all the years of study period. The Interest was highest at Rs. 526.41 lakh in the year Y_{-1} and had been increasing from year Y_0 to Y_2. Though, there had been operating losses during the period of study, there had been profits before Tax (positive) for the years Y_{-4}, Y_{-3}, Y_{-2}, and Y_0. This was because of the presence of large amounts of non-operating incomes. The non-operating income of year Y_{-1} at Rs. 1,098.18 lakh included Rs. 754.47 lakh of reliefs and remissions in terms of BIFR orders. Non-operating income was mainly in the form of interest and financial charges recovered.

Decomposition Analysis: Table – 4.4 presents component-wise analysis of total cost and Total Income. Material cost component has been around 50 per cent of the total capital. Even the other components have been by and large stable. Income from operations also had been increasing.

Table - 4.4: Decomposition of the Total Expenditure and Income of Amar Dye-Chem after the Takeover

(In Percentages)

Items \ *Years*	Y_0	Y_1	Y_2
Material	53.69	43.30	48.96
Employees	11.75	16.98	17.04
Other expenses	28.98	31.18	25.54
Interest	4.91	7.61	7.55
Depreciation	0.67	0.93	0.91

(Contd...)

I .Total Expenditure	100.00 (6256.74)	100.00 (5054.28)	100.00 (5325.90)
Income from operations	78.34	94.56	100.16
Non-Operating Income	15.78	4.02	5.66
Changes in Stock	5.88	1.42	-5.82
II .Total Income	100.00 (6,908.39)	100.00 (4,209.68)	100.00 (4,466.54)
III. Net Profit/Loss	(651.65)	(-844.60)	(-859.36)

Note: Figures within parentheses are absolute amounts in lakh of rupees.

4.4. Bokiyu Tanneries

As can be seen from Table – 4.1, the gross profit of this company was negative, except for the year Y_4. Though a decline was seen from the year Y_2, the gross loss shot upto Rs. 353.71 lakh for the year Y_3. This was mainly due to the increase in cost of goods sold. The increase of sales from year Y_2 to Y_3 is 68 per cent whereas the increase in cost of goods sold is 103 per cent. The Directors in their Annual Report to the members acknowledged this for the year Y_3, i.e., 93-94. The report says, "The above results can be considered satisfactory in view of the fact that during this period, the entire leather industry was under severe recession. Moreover there was a sharp rise in indigenous materials..." This could be better seen in decomposition analysis. The gross loss for the year Y_5, in spite of gross profit in year Y_4, could mainly be attributed to steep increase in the cost of the raw material. There was an increase of 36 per cent in the raw material cost against an increase of only 4 per cent in the sales. Similar negative trend could be observed in the operating results also with regard to profit before tax. In spite of all this there was a profit before tax. This had turned out to be a special feature of this company. This had happened mainly due to non-operating incomes. A very major component of this non-operating income was in the form of job work.

In fact, this company had been mostly depending upon job work till the time of the takeover. It is only after the takeover, the company is concentrating on its own sales.

Decomposition Analysis: The decomposition analysis also confirms the above observations. Table – 4.5 shows the decomposition of total expenditure and total income of this company.

Table – 4.5: Decomposition of Total Expenditure and Income of Bokiyu Tanneries after the Takeover

(In Percentages)

Items / *Years*	Y_0	Y_1	Y_2	Y_3	Y_4	Y_5
Material	56.64	53.94	61.29	73.38	81.28	82.71
Employees	26.08	21.46	15.51	11.48	8.81	7.62
Other Exp	6.01	10.05	6.20	5.49	5.21	3.65
Interest	9,98	12.03	13.32	7.87	3.75	5.25
Depreciation	1.29	2.52	3.68	1.78	0.95	0.77
I Total Expenditure	100.00 (237.82)	100.00 (304.90)	100.00 (617.14)	100.00 (1,152.55)	100.00 (1,719.17)	100.00 (1,974.91)
Sales	1.43	12.74	62.08	54.96	86.94	86.48
Job Work	97.25	64.56	32.57	39.45	9.71	7.64
Miscellaneous	1.58	6.45	5.78	3.39	2.43	0.96
Changes in Stock	-0.26	16.25	-0.43	2.20	0.92	4.92
II. Total Income	100.00 (160.49)	100.00 (337.43)	100.00 (657.59)	100.00 (1,251.25)	100.00 (1,961.70)	100.00 (2,006.34)
III.Net Profit/Loss	(-77.33)	(32.53)	(40.45)	(98.70)	(242.53)	(31.43)

Note: Figures within parentheses are absolute amounts in lakh of rupees.

Table – 4.5 shows that the company could manage to keep the cost of goods sold within a range of 85 per cent to 95 per cent of total cost in the post-takeover period. Though there had been a gradual increase in the cost of materials, /the company was able to manage a cut in the interest and employees costs.

Table – 4.5 also presents a picture of the components of total income. In the beginning (years Y_0 and Y_1) there had been very insignificant proportion of income from sales and a major proportion of its income came from job work. This trend had gradually changed after the takeover and the company could (Y_2 and Y_3) concentrate on its main line of activity.

4.5. India Precision Bearings

The gross profit of this company during the study period had been negative before the year of takeover (i.e. Y_{-4}, Y_{-3}, Y_{-2} and Y_{-1}) and positive in all the years after the takeover. This means that there had been a visible turnaround of the company from the year of takeover itself. If one goes through the information contained in Table - 4.1, it will be evident that a net loss of Rs. 219.00 lakh had turned into a net profit of Rs. 70.88 lakh. The EBIT also showed a similar trend as the gross profit. There had been positive EBIT from the year Y_0 onwards. The operating profit, however, had been negative for the years Y_1 and Y_3. This was mainly due to inadequate EBIT to cover the interest. The operating loss for the year Y_1 was mainly due to a higher depreciation charge of Rs. 81.24 lakh.

The profit before tax had also been showing more or less the same trend as other profits. There had been a positive PBT in spite of negative EBIT in the year Y_1. This has happened mainly due to non-operating income. From year Y_1 onwards there had been net profit, except in year Y_3. This is an evidence of the fact that the turnaround strategies, which are being implemented after the change of management, are working in the right direction. The net loss in year Y_3 was mainly due to increase in cost of material and under utilisation of installed capacity, as stated in the Directors' Report of 1992-93.

Decomposition Analysis: Table – 4.6presents an item-wise analysis of total expenditure and total income.

Table – 4.6, presents a more or less stable pattern of expenditure distribution in the post-takeover period. The interest component in year Y_0 was high at 34.32 per cent.

Subsequently it had come down to about 20 per cent and it was showing a declining trend from the year Y_3 onwards. If one observes the data in Table – 4.6 closely, one can find that there was a change in the distribution pattern of items of expenditure in the total expenditure in the year Y_6. Till the year Y_5, expenses were more than the material cost, whereas in the year Y_6, reverse had happened. The reason for this change was an increase of sales by only about 37 per cent against a steep increase of 80 per cent in material cost. The proportion of remaining expenses like interest and depreciation also were on a declining trend.

Table - 4.6: Decomposition of Total Expenditure and Income of India Precision Bearings after the Takeover

(In Percentages)

Items \ *Years*	Y_0	Y_1	Y_2	Y_3	Y_4	Y_5	Y_6
Material	26.86	33.87	25.87	29.23	28.67	35.79	47.49
Expenses	30.95	32.25	43.04	38.61	42.87	44.65	38.55
Interest	34.32	19.98	20.88	21.65	18.03	12.46	8.09
Depreciation	7.87	13.90	10.21	10.51	10.43	7.40	5.87
I Total	100.00	100.00	100.00	100.00	100.00	100.00	100.00
Expenditure	(551.10)	(584.36)	(562.02)	(570.02)	(623.52)	(895.82)	(1,220.05)
Sales	87.42	93.06	97.44	98.96	98.71	98.49	98.53
Other Incomes	6.44	9.14	2.56	1.04	1.29	1.51	1.47
Changes in Stock	6.14	-2.20	Nil	Nil	Nil	Nil	Nil
II Total	100.00	100.00	100.00	100.00	100.00	100.00	100.00
Income	(442.38)	(594.47)	(614.36)	(543.83)	(696.97)	(944.02)	(1,290.93)
III Net Profit/Loss	(-108.72)	(10.11)	(52.34)	(-26.19)	(73.45)	(48.20)	(70.88)

Note: Figures within parentheses are absolute amounts in lakh of rupees.

Table 4 – .6 also shows that most of the income is from sales. Though it was 87.42 per cent in the year Y_0, it had gradually increased to 98.71 per cent by the year Y_4. Again, in the year Y_0 the total expenditure had exceeded total income, and subsequently from year Y_1 it got reversed and the total income always had exceeded the total expenditure and has been regularly increasing, except in the year Y_3. On the whole, it can be concluded that the company is in the right direction and is in the process of turnaround.

4.6. Coromandal Pharma

The gross profit for this company had always been negative. Though in the initial year (Y_1) of the takeover the gross loss showed a slight decline, subsequently it had been continuously increasing. This tells us that the company was not responding to the turnaround efforts made by the new management. The sales were very insignificant in the years Y-1, Y_0 and Y_1. Again in the years Y_3 and Y_4 the sales were declining steadily.

It appears that, the company had attempted the turnaround with good intentions. This could be seen by the management's success in containing the gross loss for the year Y_2. Though, the sales of year Y_1 were only Rs. 0.18 lakh and the gross loss was Rs. 7.62 lakh. Whereas in the year Y_2 in spite of Rs. 248.45 lakh of sales, there had been only Rs. 23.64 lakh of gross loss. This was proportionately very less when compared with the figures of year Y_1. In the year Y_3, it seems, that the company had landed in many problems like the crash in the prices of finished goods, problems in public issue, non-availability of funds, etc. This had adversely affected the operations. The problems mentioned above of the year Y_3 continued to the year Y_4 (1995-96) also. The company was doing some job work for some time till November 1995, thereafter the operations were suspended. Now, the company was approaching BIFR with fresh rehabilitation scheme.

Decomposition Analysis: Table - 4.7 presents a picture of total cost and total income.

Table - 4.7: Decomposition of Total Expenditure and Income of Coromandal Pharma after the Takeover

(In Percentages)

Items \ *Years*	Y_0	Y_1	Y_2	Y_3	Y_4
Materials	1.12	12.83	55.44	13.95	18.25
Employees	5.49	15.68	3.37	6.67	5.60
Other Expenses	13.12	31.13	18.47	37.08	31.62
Interest	71.54	32.52	16.68	33.68	36.71
Depreciation	8.73	7.84	6.04	8.62	7.82
I Total Expenditure	100.00 (72.43)	100.00 (16.45)	100.00 (352.09)	100.00 (308.38)	100.00 (239.38)
Sales	9.60	5.33	88.54	91.01	1394
Other Incomes	90.58	39.94	0.11	2.89	299
Changes in Stock	-0.18	54.73	11.35	6.10	-1593
II Total Income	100.00 (11.59)	100.00 (3.38)	100.00 (280.61)	100.00 (83.31)	100.00 (34.88)
III Net Profit/Loss	(-61.07)	(-13.07)	(-71.48)	(-225.07)	(-204.50)

Note: Figures within parentheses are absolute amounts in lakh of rupees

It was evident from Table – 4.7 that the material cost had been mostly (excepting the years Y_0 and Y_2) between 10 per cent and 20 per cent of the total cost. The employee costs were more or less stable at around 5 per cent. Nevertheless if one closely observed the trends of various cost figures, it was very erratic. To some extent this phenomenon could also be seen in years Y_3 and Y_4, where the sales were relatively less. Only the expenditure on the depreciation was stable during the post-takeover period. Total costs were many times higher than the total income in majority years of the study period. The net losses had been several times higher than the total income. It was evident from the above analysis that this company could not turnaround in spite of management change.

Table – 4.7 also shows the decomposition of total income of Coromandal Pharma. The total income was very insignificant during the study period except for the years Y_2 and Y_3. Only in these two years, there had been an income of about 90 per cent from sales and in the remaining years the income from sales was insignificant. In the year Y_4, there was very little income after adjusting for the changes in stocks. From this analysis, it can be concluded that this company was in a serious financial problems and incurring heavy losses even after the takeover. Therefore, the turnaround through takeover could be said to be a failure in this case.

4.7. Mico Farm Chemicals

The gross profit had been positive from the first year of the takeover (y_1) itself. Another interesting issue was that there had been an increase in the gross profit, in spite of reduced sales in the year Y_5 when compared to the year Y_4. The reduction in sales was attributed to lower demand for one of its products and the impending ban on one of the products. EBIT followed the same trend as gross profit. However, in the operating profit, there had been operating losses in the years Y_2 and Y_3. This was because of the surplus generated, in the form of EBIT, was not sufficient to meet the interest burden of the firm for these years. Finally, the company could manage a positive PBT from year Y_1, with the help of sizable amounts of non-operating income, which included a major portion from stock valuation adjustments.

Decomposition Analysis: Table – 4.8 presents the decomposition of the components of total expenditure and total income.

Table -4.8 shows a steady increase in sales except in the year Y_3. The material cost component had been high in the year Y_2 and declining since then. The employee cost maintained a stable proportion at around 5 per cent of the total cost. The other costs were highest at 35 per cent in year Y_5. This had happened owing to an increase in the fuel and consumables, repairs and maintenance and discounts and rebates. This increase had been compensated by a decrease in the material cost component.

Table – 4.8: Decomposition of the Total Expenditure and Income of Mico Farm Chemicals after the Takeover

(In percentages)

Items \ Years	Y_0	Y_1	Y_2	Y_3	Y_4	Y_5
Material Cost	50.18	62.60	68.89	60.46	60.45	50.48
Employees Cost	4.28	4.18	3.56	4.45	5.14	5.67
Other Costs	33.98	20.90	17.95	25.12	26.87	34.68
Financial Expenses	6.40	10.92	8.61	8.42	6.24	7.82
Depreciation	5.16	1.40	0.99	1.55	1.30	1.35
I Total Expenditure	100.00 (290.05)	100.00 (595.39)	100.00 (1066.75)	100.00 (989.65)	100.00 (1366.95)	100.00 (1216.31)
Operating Income	70.29	111.01	96.10	88.16	100.12	98.80
Non Operating Income	0.10	0.74	0.86	3.63	3.08	2.22
Changes in stocks	29.61	-11.75	3.04	8.21	-3.20	-1.02
II Total Income	100.00 (244.52)	100.00 (600.23)	100.00 (1067.97)	100.00 (1030.24)	100.00 (1452.39)	100.00 (1380.23)
III Net Profit/ Loss	(-45.53)	(4.84)	(1.22)	(40.59)	(85.44)	(163.92)

Note: Figures within parentheses are absolute amounts in lakh of rupees.

Table – 4.8 also shows that most of income was from operations. However, in some of the years the effect of changes in stocks on the total income had been very significant. The total income had always been on an increasing trend, except in the year Y_5. The difference between total cost and total income, i.e., net profit (loss) was also positive. There had been a regular and increasing amount of profits except in the year Y_2.

4.8. Sivamani Spinning

As stated earlier, the information was available for this

company for the years Y_{-4}, Y_{-3}, Y_{-2}, Y_2, Y_3 and Y_4. In addition to this, it was not possible to get Income and Expenditure Account of this company for the years Y_{-4}, Y_{-3} and Y_{-2}. Therefore only net profit (loss) figures were available for these years.

After the takeover, the gross profit had been positive at Rs.51.97 lakh in the years Y_2 and it had reached a maximum of Rs.75.49 lakh by the year Y_3, before it declined to Rs.40.14 lakh by the very next year, i.e., Y_4.

EBIT also followed the same trend as gross profit for the years Y_2, Y_3 and Y_4. The contribution towards depreciation had been declining from the year Y_2 to Y_4. There had been operating losses for the years Y_2 and Y_4 and operating profit for the year Y_3 at Rs.23.36 lakh. The interest burden for this period had been steady for years Y_2 and Y_3 and increased to Rs.25.77 lakh.

The net profit/loss was seen for the years Y_{-4}, Y_{-3}, Y_{-2} and Y_4. This means that there had been net profits in the years Y_2 and Y_3 after the takeover and again the company entered into losses phase from the year Y_4.

Decomposition Analysis: Table – 4.9 presents the decomposition of total expenditure and total income.

It can be seen from Table – 4.9 that there had been a steady increase in the total expenditure. Cost of material also had been gradually increasing, whereas production expenses were following a mixed trend. The other expenses, interest charges and depreciation were on a declining trend over the period of study. This can be considered a healthy sign.

It may be seen from Table - 4.9 that more than 95 per cent of the income was from business operations. More specifically, it had been varying between 96 per cent and 99 per cent during the period of study. The non-operating income was at a nominal level with a maximum of a little over 3 per cent. On the whole, the total income has been on an increasing trend over this period from year to year. The gap between the total income and total expenditure also had been positive for the years Y_2 and Y_3 and negative for Year Y_4.

Table – 4.9: Decomposition of the Total Expenditure and Income of Sivamani Spinning after the Takeover

(In Percentages)

Items / *Years*	Y_2	Y_3	Y_4
Material Cost	53.36	61.21	66.49
Production Expenses	8.42	5.61	4.65
Other Expenses	5.96	4.62	4.53
Depreciation	11.42	7.15	4.47
I Total Expenditure	100.00	100.00	100.00
	(343.55)	(443.07)	(548.60)
Operating Income	96.38	99.10	98.85
Miscellaneous Income	3.62	0.90	1.15
II Total Income	100.00	100.00	100.00
	(348.44)	(470.66)	(544.74)
III Net Profit/Loss	(4.89)	(27.59)	(-3.86)

Note: Figures within parentheses are absolute amounts in lakh of rupees.

5. ANALYSIS THROUGH RATIOS

In this section, it is proposed to study the profitability performance of the selected units during the study period through the ratios and proportions. More specifically, the following ratios had been used for the analysis.

1. Cost of Goods Sold to Total Cost
2. Cost of Goods Sold to Sales
3. Total Cost to Sales
4. Total Cost to Total Income
5. Net Profit (loss) to Total Income
6. Return On Investment

5.1. Cost of Goods Sold to Total Cost

This ratio would tell us the extent of cost of goods sold to total cost. The remaining percentage of total cost is non-operating costs, which has no direct bearing on the production. In other words, this ratio would tell us what was the proportions of cost of goods sold and the other costs in the total cost. Table–4.10 shows the company-wise and year-wise data of cost of goods sold to total cost.

Table – 4.10: Cost of Goods Sold as a percentage of Total Cost of the Sample Units after the Takeover

(In Percentages)

Companies \ Years	Y_0	Y_1	Y_2	Y_3	Y_4	Y_5	Y_6
Dempo Dairy	82.27	56.41	77.38	86.54	NA	x	x
ICML	8.32	91.59	91.66	96.39	97.57	x	x
Amar Dye-Chem	94.42	91.46	91.54	x	x	x	x
Bokiyu Tanneries	88.73	85.45	83.00	90.35	95.30	93.98	x
India Precision	57.81	66.12	68.91	67.84	71.54	80.44	86.04
Coromandal Pharma	19.73	59.52	77.28	57.70	55.47	x	x
Mico Farm Chemical	88.44	87.68	90.40	90.03	92.46	90.83	x
Sivamani Spinning	NA	NA	82.62	88.23	91.00	NA	x

Notes: 'NA' indicates data not available.
'x' indicates years beyond year Y_n.

Table – 4.10 reveals that the cost of goods sold is more than 80 per cent of the total cost in the following companies in all the years:

a. ICML

b. Amar Dye-Chem

c. Bokiyu Tanneries

d. Mico Farm Chemicals

e. Sivamani Spinning

In case of ICML, there had been no sales for the year Y_0 and consequently, there was insignificant cost of goods sold. Therefore, this figure had not been considered in this analysis.

For Dempo Dairy, there had been a steady increase in the proportion of cost of goods sold after the takeover. In case of India Precision this ratio had started with about 58 per cent and reached a maximum of about 86 per cent by the year Y_6, with regular and steady increases from year to year. Coromandal Pharma had ratios between 55 per cent and 80 per cent of cost of goods sold to total cost. This implied that their cost of production was less and expenditure on items like interest and depreciation are high. In the case of Coromandal Pharma the sales was generally less and gradually decreasing. But the interest cost and depreciation had remained more or less stable. This had led to a decline in the proportion of cost of goods sold to total cost from year Y_3 onwards. It is generally concluded that reducing the proportions of non-operating costs in the total cost would be in the interest of the company.

5.2. Cost of Goods Sold to Sales

This ratio tells the relation among the cost of goods sold, gross profit (loss) and net sales. Generally, if the proportion of cost of goods sold was less than a hundred per cent then, there would be a gross profit and if it was more than a hundred per cent, there would be a gross loss. Table – 4.11 presents a picture of cost of goods sold to sales in percentages.

On examing data in Table – 4.11, one can classify the sample units into three groups. They are:

1. Companies, which had always less than a hundred per cent cost of goods sold to sales, after year Y_1, like:
   a. Dempo Dairy
   b. ICML
   c. India Precision
   d. Mico Farm chemicals
   e. Sivamani spinning

2. Companies, which had always more than a hundred per cent of cost of goods sold to sales, after year Y_1, like:

   a. Amar Dye-Chem.

   b. Coromandal Pharma, and

3. Companies, which had a mixed trend:

   a. Bokiyu Tanneries.

Table – 4.11: Cost of Goods Sold as a percentage of Sales of Sample Companies after the Takeover

(In Percentages)

Companies \ Years	Y_0	Y_1	Y_2	Y_3	Y_4	Y_5	Y_6
Dempo Dairy	85.50	56.49	74.67	77.99	NA	x	x
ICML	+	96.45	81.89	90.73	94.78	x	x
Amar Dye-Chem	109.15	116.13	108.98	x	x	x	x
Bokiyu Tanneries	+	605.88	125.46	151.44	96.06	106.96	x
India Precision	82.37	64.54	64.70	71.86	64.84	77.51	82.53
Coromandal Pharma	+	+	109.51	168.78	291.96	x	x
Mico Farm Chemicals	149.24	78.35	93.96	98.09	86.92	81.01	x
Sivamani Spinning	NA	NA	84.52	83.82	92.55	NA	x

Notes: 'NA' indicates data not available, 'x' indicates years beyond year Y_n, and

'+' indicates no sales or very insignificant sales.

In other words, companies included in the first category are the units with gross profit, and in the category second are the companies with gross losses and the units in the third category are with sometimes-gross profits and sometimes with gross losses.

5.3. Total Cost to Sales

This ratio tells the relation among the total cost, operating profit (loss) and sales. The yardstick, here, was that if the ratio was more than a hundred per cent, there were operating losses and if it was less than a hundred per cent, there was operating profit. Table - 4.12 presents a picture of this ratio over the post-takeover period.

Table - 4.12: Total Expenditure as a percentage of Net Sales of Sample Companies after the Takeover

(In Percentages)

Years / Companies	Y_0	Y_1	Y_2	Y_3	Y_4	Y_5	Y_6
Dempo Dairy	103.93	119.08	96.51	90.11	NA	x	x
ICML	+	105.30	89.35	94.12	97.14	x	x
Amar Dye-Chem.	115.61	126.97	119.05	x	x	x	x
Bokiyu Tanneries	+	709.07	151.17	167.61	100.80	113.82	x
India Precision	142.50	105.63	93.88	105.92	90.63	96.35	95.92
Coromandal Pharma	+	+	141.71	406.83	719.19	x	x
Mico Farm Chemcals	168.75	89.36	103.94	108.96	94.01	89.19	x
Sivamani Spinning	NA	NA	102.30	94.99	101.88	NA	x

Notes: 'NA' indicates data not available, 'x' indicates years beyond year Y_n, and
'+' indicates no sales or very insignificant sales.

On examining data in Table – 4.12, one can classify the sample companies into two groups. They are:

1. Companies, which have always more than a hundred per cent ratio, like:
   a. Amar Dye - Chem
   b. Bokiyu Tanneries
   c. Coromandal Pharma, and
2. Companies, which have a blend of both more than and less than a hundred per cent ratio during the study period like:
   a. Dempo Dairy
   b. ICML

c. India Precision

d. Mico Farm Chemicals

e. Sivamani Spinning

In other words, companies in the first group always had operating losses and in the second group had a blend of both operating profits and operating losses variously. On further analysis of the trends, one can classify the companies into four categories. They are:

1. Companies, which have improved the position by converting operating losses into operating profits:

    a. Dempo Dairy

    b. ICML

2. Companies with a mixed trend:

    a. India Precision

    b. Mico Farm Chemicals

    c. Sivamani Spinning

3. Companies where the operating loss is not following any trend:

    a. Amar Dye-Chem

    b. Bokiyu Tanneries and

4. Companies with increasing operating losses year after year:

    a. Coromandal Pharma

It could be concluded from the above analysis that all units except the Amar Dye-Chem, Bokiyu Tanneries and Coromandal Pharma, were earning operating profits after the takeover. It implied that the companies had turned around after the takeover.

5.4 Total Cost to Total Income

This ratio analyses the relation among total cost, total

income and profit before tax. The guiding principle here is that if the ratio is less than hundred percent, it results in net profit and if it is more than a hundred per cent, the company suffers a net loss. Table - 4.13 shows the company-wise and year-wise analysis of this ratio.

Table-4.13: Total Expenditure as a percentage of Total Income of Sample Companies after the Takeover

(In Percentages)

Company \ Years	Y_0	Y_1	Y_2	Y_3	Y_4	Y_5	Y_6
Dempo Dairy	127.41	109.86	85.33	83.85	NA	x	x
ICML	+	94.40	93.20	95.11	96.33	x	x
Amar Dye-Chem.	90.57	120.06	119.24	x	x	x	x
Bokiyu Tanneries	148.18	90.36	93.85	92.11	87.64	98.43	x
India Precision	124.58	98.30	91.48	104.82	89.46	94.89	94.51
Coromandal Pharma	637.59	486.69	125.47	370.16	x	x	x
Mico Farm Chemicals	118.62	99.19	99.89	96.06	94.12	88.13	x
Sivamani Spinning	NA	NA	98.60	94.14	100.71	NA	x

Notes: 'NA' indicates data not available, 'x' indicates years beyond year Y_n, and
'+' indicates no sales or very insignificant sales.

Basing on the information contained in Table - 4.13, the sample companies can be classified into three categories as follows:

1. Companies, which have always less than a hundred per cent ratio after the takeover:
   a. Dempo Dairy
   b. ICML
   c. Bokiyu Tanneries
   d. Mico Farm Chemicals
2. Companies with more than a hundred per cent ratio after the takeover:

a. Amar Dye-Chem

b. Coromandal Pharma, and

3. Companies with a mixed trend:

a. India Precision

b. Sivamani Spinning

5.5. Net Profit to Total Income

This ratio explains the proportion of net profit to the total income. If the ratio was positive, there was a net profit and if it is negative, it indicated a net loss. Table – 4.14 presents the relevant information.

Table – 4.14: Net Profit as a percentage of Total Income of Sample Companies after the Takeover

(In Percentages)

Companies \ Years	Y_0	Y_1	Y_2	Y_3	Y_4	Y_5	Y_6
Dempo Dairy	-	-	14.67	16.15	NA	x	x
ICML	+	5.60	6.80	4.89	3.77	x	x
Amar Dye-Chem	9.43	-	-	x	x	x	x
Bokiyu Tanneries	-	9.64	6.15	7.89	12.36	1.57	x
India Precision	-	1.70	8.52	-	10.54	5.11	5.57
Coromandal Pharma	+	+	+	+	+	x	x
Mico Farm Chemicals	-	0.81	0.11	3.94	5.88	11.87	x
Sivamani Spinning	NA	NA	1.40	5.86	-	NA	x

Notes: 'A' indicates data not available, 'x' indicates years beyond year Y_n,
'+' indicates the Insignificant income, and
'-' indicates there was net loss in that year

After going through the Table – 4.14 one can classify the companies under study into four categories. They are:

1. Companies, which started with net losses and entered into net profit phase after the takeover such as:

   a. Dempo Dairy
   b. ICML
   c. Bokiyu Tanneries
   d. Mico Farm Chemicals

2. Company, which incurred net losses, even after the takeover, like:
   a. Coromandal pharma
3. Company with fluctuations in profits and losses:
   a. Indian Precision
4. Companies which had started with profits but got into losses later, such as:
   a. Amar Dye-Chem
   b. Sivamani Spinning

5.6. Return On Investment

ROI is generally considered to be a comprehensive measure of computing profitability of any company, since it is the product of two other significant ratios, viz., asset turnover and profit margin. The total sample units had been divided into two groups based on the changes in EBIT after the takeover. They are: (1) Companies with a positive return after the takeover and (2) Companies with no positive return even after the takeover. Since the study includes only companies that were referred to BIFR, there was no possibility of positive return before the takeover. Hence, this part of the study was mainly focused on the post-takeover period and the respective returns, it should not be concluded that there was no turnaround if there was no positive return. This is because even a decline in the negative return could be considered as a sign of turnaround. The classification attempted in this section was only to calculate Return On Investment (ROI) but not to categorize them as turnaround companies and non-turnaround companies.

There are five companies under Category - I and three

companies in Category - II, as shown in Tables -4.15 and 4.16 respectively. In case of companies shown in Table - 4.15, there had been positive and regular ROI in majority of the years after the takeover. In addition to these, there might also be some companies in Table – 4.16 that had reduced their losses over the period of study and hence are on the threshold of turnaround.

5.6.1. Category-I Companies: A detailed analysis of companies included in this category is presented below:

Table - 4.15: Return on Investment* of the Sample Units after the Takeover

Companies	*Items* \ *Years*	Y_0	Y_1	Y_2	Y_3	Y_4	Y_5	Y_6
Dempo Dairy	Asset Turnover (Times)	1.49	0.47	0.62	1.36	NA	x	x
	Profit Margin (%)	+	+	20.96	12.69	NA	x	x
	ROI (%)	+	+	13.00	17.25	NA	x	x
ICML	Asset Turnover (times)	-	1.43	2.58	2.72	2.72	x	x
	Profit Margin (%)	+	2.78	17.43	8.89	4.91	x	x
	ROI (%)	+	3.98	44.97	24.18	13.36	x	x
India Precision	Asset Turnover (times)	0.40	0.49	0.42	0.39	0.48	0.58	0.80
	Profit Margin (%)	6.41	15.48	25.72	17.01	25.71	15.37	11.83
	ROI (%)	2.56	7.59	10.80	6.63	12.34	8.91	9.46

(Contd...)

	Asset Turnover (times)	0.56	1.33	1.49	1.31	1.55	1.28	x
Mico Farm Chemicals	Profit Margin (%)	+	9.82	5.01	0.22	10.50	15.88	x
	ROI (%)	+	13.06	7.46	0.29	16.28	20.33	x
	Asset Turnover (times)	NA	NA	1.48	1.94	1.56	NA	x
Sivamani Spinning	Profit Margin (%)	NA	NA	3.20	7.85	2.90	NA	x
	ROI (%)	NA	NA	4.74	15.23	4.52	NA	x

Notes: '+' indicates no positive EBIT for that year.
NA indicates data not available.
'X' indicates years beyond year Y_n.
'-' Indicates no sales for that year.
* ROI is not calculated for the companies with negative EBIT all over the study period.

Dempo Dairy: There was no positive EBIT for years Y_0 and Y_1 in this company and therefore the profit margin and ROI could not be calculated. From year Y_2, there had been a positive EBIT. The asset turnover was only 0.62 times and profit margin was 20.96 per cent making an overall ROI of 13 per cent. But in year Y_3, the asset turnover was 1.36 times and profit margin was 12.69 per cent making an overall ROI of 17.25 per cent. The reason for less profit margin in year Y_3 was that for an increase of 134 per cent of sales there was an increase of only 42 per cent of profit. This had reduced the profit margin drastically. Similarly, the increase of sales and more or less the same amount of total assets was the reason for tremendous increase in the asset turnover from 0.62 to 1.36 times in the year Y_3. This increase in asset turnover has improved the ROI of Y_3 inspite of lower profit margin.

ICML: In this case, there was no sales in the year Y_0, consequently, asset turnover, profit margin and ROI could not be calculated. The asset turnover of this company has been increasing though there was no change in it for year Y_3 and Y_4. However, the profit margin had been continuously declining from year Y_2 onwards. The ROI was also following the same trend as of profit margin. One interesting observation is that the ROI was about 45 per cent in year Y_2 that was mainly because of high profit margin and asset turnover.

India Precision: In this case, the asset turnover was always less than one time, (in fact it was less than 0.5 time till the year Y_4) in all the years of the study period. However, the profit margin had been steadily growing with an exception of year Y_3 till year Y_4. Thereafter, even the profit margin had showed a declining trend in the years Y_5 and Y_6. The ROI also, though showed a gradual improvement till the year Y_3, started declining in the year Y_5 and the ROI for the years Y_5 and Y_6 was less than the ROI of Y_4. This was because of the reason that the profit margin had showed a declining trend in spite of increasing asset turnover. Therefore, the company should improve profit margin. In spite of higher sales, the interest and depreciation expenses were by and large stable. The company was not in a position to improve its profits, particularly in the years Y_5 and Y_6. This could be mainly attributed to the increases in the cost of goods sold.

Mico Farm Chemicals: In this case there was negative EBIT, for the year Y_0 and consequently, there was no profit margin and no ROI for that year. Though the asset turnover was more than 1 time, but there had been no trend emerging. The profit margin was the lowest at 0.22 per cent in the year Y_3. The ROI also followed the same trend as profit margin. The reason for this was the decline in the sales and consequent decline in the profits as explained in the previous sections.

Sivamani Spinning: In this case, the asset turnover had been between 1.5 and 2.0 times during the study period. The profit margin also, had increased from year Y_2 to Y_3, but declined in the year Y_4 to an all-time low of 2.90 per cent. Consequently, the ROI also followed the same trend as profit margin. The reason for the decline in the ROI was both a decline in the asset turnover and a steep decline in the profit margin. Naturally, the ROI declined as a result of these two changes.

5.6.2. Category-II Companies: These were the companies where there was no positive EBIT in all or most of the years of study period. As indicated earlier, there were three companies in this category as shown in Table - 4.16. In two cases, there had been a mixed trend with frequent increases and decreases whereas the other company, viz., Coromandal Pharma had an ever-increasing negative EBIT from the year Y_1 onwards.

Table - 4.16 : List of Companies with Negative EBIT all over the Post-takeover Period

Years / *Companies*	Y_0	Y_1	Y_2	Y_3	Y_4	Y_5
Amar Dye-Chem						
EBIT (Rs. in lakh)	-131.04	-652.12	-450.06	x	x	x
Asset turnover (Times)	1.08	0.90	1.15	x	x	x
Bokiyu Tanneries						
EBIT (Rs. in lakh)	-211.79	-225.21	-126.67	-374.2	50.92	-136.04
Asset Turnover (Times)	0.03	0.19	0.54	0.75	0.97	0.77
Coromandal Pharma						
EBIT (Rs. in lakh)	-19.52	-7.13	-35.94	-52.49	-71.29	x
Asset Turnover (Times)	0.01	+	0.45	0.11	0.05	x

Notes: 'x' indicates years beyond year Y_n

'+' Indicates positive but very insignificant figure.

Amar Dye-Chem: This unit had only two years of post-takeover performance. There had been only negative EBIT in all the years even after the takeover. However, the EBIT had showed a better performance by reducing the negative balance of EBIT in the year Y_2. Even, the asset turnover was following the same trend. There was a sudden increase in the negative EBIT from Rs.131.04 lakh in the year Y_0 to Rs.652.12 lakh in the year Y_1. This had happened because of the reason that there had been a decrease in sales of year Y_1 by 26 per cent, whereas, the cost of goods sold had reduced only by 17 per cent.

Bokiyu Tanneries: There had been always negative EBIT in all the years except in the year Y_4 and the EBIT was not following any trend over the study period. There had been increases and decreases in EBIT, over these years. However, the asset turnover had always been less than 1 time and continuously increasing except in year Y_5. Another interesting observation was that the cost of goods sold had always been more than the net sales except in the year Y_4. It was for this reason that the company was not able to come out from the red.

Coromandal Pharma: In this case, the loss before interest had been continuously increasing, except in year Y_1. The asset turnover had always been very insignificant except for the year Y_2, where the asset turnover ratio was 0.45 times. The sales during the entire study period were insignificant except for the year Y_2.

PART - II

It is intended to test the following two hypotheses in this section:

1. The companies that were taken over by the better-known industrial groups shall turnaround faster than those that were taken over by the relatively lesser - known groups or individuals.
2. When a takeover of a sick company takes place, the taken over company, with the support of the taking over company, shall try to expand or modernise their business activities in the process of their turning around.

I. In order to test the validity of the **first hypothesis** given above, the sample companies have been divided into two groups.

The two groups are: (1) units taken over by better-known managements and (2) the units taken over by lesser-known managements. Table - 4.17 presents the details of each of the two groups of companies.

Table - 4.17: Group-Wise List of Sample Units and their Taken over Managements

Sl. No.	*Name of the Sample Unit*	*Taken over by*
Group - I		
1.	Dempo Dairy Industries Ltd.	Karnataka Milk Federation National Dairy Development Board
2.	Industrial Chemicals and Monomers Ltd. (ICML)	India Cements Ltd.
3.	Bokiyu Tanneries Ltd.	MESCO group
4.	India Precision Bearings Mfrs. Ltd.	Lakshmi Machinery Works Ltd.
5.	Mico Farm Chemicals Ltd.	South India Viscose Ltd.
Group - II		
1.	Amar Dye-Chem Ltd.	Mr. R.S. Mardia & Associates
2.	Coramandal Pharmaceuticals Ltd.	Mr.C.V. Krishna Rao & Others
3.	Sivamani Spinning and Weavings Mills Ltd.	Mr. Thiagarajan

In case of all the above 5 units of Group - I, the taken over managements are well diversified and known in their respective industry and are in good health. The remaining three units of Group - II were taken over by relatively lesser-known Management. An attempt is made in this section to study the validity of the first hypothesis in respect of the above two groups of sample units with the help of a comparison of certain parameters between the period Y_o and Y_n.

6. LIQUIDITY PARAMETERS

Under this section, liquidity of these two groups of companies is measured and compared, with the parameters like of Current and Quick Ratios, Net Working Capital, and Diversion of Funds as shown in Table – 4.18.

Table - 4.18: A Comparison of Liquidity Parameters of Sample Units between the Years Y_o and Y_n

Companies taken over by	*Current Ratio*		*Quick Ratio*		*Net Working Capital*		*Diversion of Short-term Funds to Long-term Uses*
	Y_o	Y_n	Y_o	Y_n	Y_o	Y_n	
	(Times)		*(Times)*		*(Rs. in Lakh)*		*(Rs. in Lakh)*
Better-known Mgts							
Dempo Dairy	0.70	2.53	0.06	1.72	-20.00	144.00	NIL
ICML	0.22	2.29	0.13	1.81	-163.62	348.98	NIL
Bokiyu Tanneries	0.34	1.11	0.16	0.83	-135.53	187.14	NIL
India Precision	0.98	2.33	0.36	0.95	-7.65	410.12	NIL
Mico Farm Chem	3.30	1.44	1.49	1.13	134.85	304.72	NIL
Less-known Mgts							
Amar Dye-Chem	0.89	0.48	0.45	0.26	-446.33	-2,963.37	2,517.04
Coramandal Pha	0.08	1.08	0.08	1.01	-104.32	24.76	NIL
Sivamani Spin	0.19+	0.77	0.12+	0.42	-54.40+	-73.99	129.08

Note: '+' indicates data for year Y_{-2}, as data for Y_o was not available.

6.1. Current and Quick Ratios

The current and quick ratios were less than 1 time and 0.5 times respectively in the year Y_o, in all the sample units except in case of Mico Farm Chemicals. However, by the year Y_n the current ratio had improved and a majority of the units under better-known Management had a ratio of more than the standard of 2 times. Whereas in case of majority of the companies under lesser-known Management, the ratio was still less than 1 time.

Similarly, the Quick Ratio also improved in a majority of the companies under better-known Managements to more than 1 time in the year Y_n. But a majority of the companies had a quick ratio of less than 0.5 times even in the year Y_n. Therefore, it is evident that the companies under better - known Managements are turning around better and faster.

6.2. Net Working Capital

Among the companies taken over by better-known Managements, there was negative networking capital in four companies out of the five companies in the year Y_o, and in one unit, there was positive Net Working Capital. However, by the year Y_n all the companies had a positive net working capital. In the second group of units (the units taken over by lesser-known Managements), there was negative net working capital in all the three companies in the year Y_o and the same position continued till Y_n with increasing magnitude. From this data the conclusion that emerges is that those units taken over by the relatively better-known Managements turned around better than the companies taken over by relatively lesser-known Managements. In fact, majority of units taken over by lesser-known Managements had deteriorated in their net working capital position by the year Y_n.

6.3. Diversion of Funds from Short-term Sources to Long-term Uses

In the first group of companies, not even a single unit had diversified its funds from short-term sources to long-term uses. This diversion is considered as an unhealthy practice. However, in the second group except Coramandal Pharma, the other two units had diverted short-term funds for long-term uses.

7. LEVERAGE PARAMETERS

In this section, leverage of the two groups of units are tested with the parameters like Total Debt and Equity to Total Assets, Total Borrowings and Equity to EBITD and Interest Coverage Ratios, in order to verify the validity or otherwise of the proposition. Table – 4.19, presents the data on these parameters.

Table – 4.19: A comparison of Leverage Parameters of the Sample Units between the Years Y_0 and Y_n

(Times)

Companies taken over by	*T.D. and Equity to Total Assets*		*Total Borrowing and Equity to EBITD*		*Interest Coverage Ratio*	
	Y_0	Y_n	Y_0	Y_n	Y_0	Y_n
Better-known Mgts:						
Dempo Dairy	3.29	1.65	Negative (EBITD)	4.13	0.70	2.20
ICML	6.47	1.64	Negative	9.79	Negative (EBIT)	2.40
Bokiyu Tanneries	4.91	0.84	Negative	12.67	Negative	Negative
India Precision	2.00	1.36	15.69	8.93	0.13	1.53
Mico Farm Chemicals	1.64	0.99	Negative	4.30	Negative	2.55
Lesser-known Mgts:						
Amar Dye-Chem	1.43	2.08	7.17	Negative	Negative	Negative
Coramandal Pharma	4.21	1.49	Negative	Negative	Negative	Negative
Sivamani Spinning	1.78+	1.54	7.43+	11.45	0.62+	0.61

Notes: 'Negative' indicates negative EBIT or EBITD, which ever is applicable

'+' Indicates the data for year Y_2, as the data for year Y_0 was not available

7.1. Total Debt and Equity to Total Assets

This ratio indicates the extent of assets coverage of total debt and equity. Normally, the total assets should be more than the total of debt and equity, as a result of reserves and surpluses and, therefore, this ratio should be less than 1 time. From the Table - 4.19, it may be seen that all the sample companies have brought down this ratio from the year Y_0 to Y_n, except in Amar Dye-Chem. With regard to the two cases other than the Amar Dye-Chem under the lesser-known Management, all the variables: the assets, the equity and the debt, are increasing and since the increase in assets was more, the ratio could be brought down. It may be concluded that these two units could not generate the profit in spite of the increase in assets, thereby could not turnaround effectively.

7.2. Total Borrowing and Equity to EBITD

This ratio is a relationship between the earnings available before interest, taxes and depreciation to the repaying obligations of a company. The ratio should be positive and the lower the ratio is, the better the firms are. Except for three units there was negative EBITDs in all the units in the year Y_o. However, by the year Y_n all the units under the category of companies taken over by better-known Managements have positive ratios. On the other hand, two out of the three companies under lesser-known managements have negative EBITDs in the year Y_n also, which is not a healthy sign. The remaining one unit under this category has also increased this ratio from year Y_o to Y_n, which is also not a healthy sign. The units under better-known Managements have made positive EBITDs and reduced this ratio from year Y_o to Y_n. The conclusion emerging from this ratio is that the units under better-known Managements have better proportion between the EBITD and the total of borrowings and debt.

7.3. Interest Coverage Ratio

This ratio is a relationship between EBIT and interest charges. This ratio indicates by how many times the EBIT is able to cover the interest obligation of the companies. The higher the ratio, the better the company's position is. In the year Y_o, there was no positive EBIT for a majority of the sample units and hence no ratio. However, by the year Y_n all the units except Bokiyu Tanneries, under better-known Managements had positive and better ratios. On the other hand, two units under the lesser-known Managements continued with negative EBITs and the third unit had a reduced ratio, which was not a healthy trend. On the whole, it may be concluded that most of the companies under better-known Managements had turned around with better and positive ratios and the units under lesser-known Managements could not turnaround, with continued negative EBIT and decreasing interest coverage ratios.

8. OTHER PARAMETERS

In this section a comparison was made between these two groups of units with the help of certain other parameters like Sales Performance, Net worth, ROI and Total Assets, which were shown in Table - 4.20.

8.1. Sales Performance

From Table - 4.20, it can be seen that the sales in case of units under better-known Managements have improved by manifold from the year Y_o to Y_n. Similarly, in two units out of the three, even in case of units under relatively lesser-known Managements have also improved their sales. The only exception to this is Amar Dye-Chem, which has registered a decline in sales from the year Y_o to Y_n.

8.2. Return on Investment

In the year Y_o, all the units under study had negative ROIs, except in India Precision Bearings. However, by the year Y_n, the units under better-known Managements have registered positive ROIs except in the case of Bokiyu Tanneries. The units under lesser-known Managements continued with their negative ROIs even in the year Y_n, except in case of Sivamani Spinning. These units have not only continued with their negative ROIs but had increased the negative balance of EBIT in the Year Y_n in comparison to Year Y_o.

Therefore, it may be concluded that the units under better-known Managements had better ROIs after the takeover. Though some of the units under lesser-known Managements have improved their sales performance but could not produce better ROIs.

Table - 4.20: A Comparison of Other Parameters of Sample Units between the Years Y_o and Y_n

Companies	*Sales Performance*		*ROI*		*Net worth*		*Total Assets*	
Taken over by	Y_o	Y_n	Y_o	Y_n	Y_o	Y_n	Y_o	Y_n
	(Rs. in lakh)		*(In % ages)*		*(Rs. in lakh)*		*(Rs. in lakh)*	
Better-know Mgts:								
Dempo Dairy	407.00	536.00	Negative	17.25	-520.00	-163.00	269.00	395.00
ICML	-	2042.95	Negative	13.36	-563.30	-256.14	120.50	750.67
Bokiyu Tanneries	2.29	1735.12	-211.79	-136.04	-307.10	389.77	91.26	2260.81
India Precision	386.75	1271.93	2.56	9.46	-671.03	-273.48	971.18	1581.18
Mico Farm Chemicals	171.88	1363.73	Negative	20.33	-129.29	107.56	308.58	1196.93
Lesser-know Mgts:								
Amar Dye-Chem	5412.02	4473.54	-131.04	-450.06	72.83	-1975.27	5017.72	3883.14
Coramandal Pharma	1.09	43.08	-19.52	-71.29	-308.92	-244.23	107.30	880.27
Sivamani Spinning	-	538.46	Negative	4.52	-42.32	-86.38	241.79	345.28

Note: '-' indicates no sales or insignificant sales.

8.3. Net Worth

Net worth can be considered as a better indicator of a company's turnaround, since the units included in the sample are basically sick units. All the sample companies with an exception of Amar Dye-Chem had negative net worths in the year Y_o. However, by the year Y_n, the companies under better-known Managements had either reduced their negative balances or had registered positive net worths. In contrast, units under lesser-known Managements had increased their negative net worths, except in case of Coramandal Pharma. However, a little deeper analysis shows that the Coramandal Pharma had a positive net worth in the year Y_1, as a result of more total assets than the total of debt and equity. However, this positive net worth had vanished by the next year and the negative net worth kept on increasing. Therefore, even this company had not really reduced the negative balance of net worth. It is concluded, that the companies under better-known Managements have improved their net worth from year Y_o to Y_n.

8.4. Total Assets

All the sample units had increased their total assets from the year Y_o to Y_n, except Amar Dye-Chem. However, the increase in assets could not help in improving the ROI of the firms under lesser-known Managements.

II. **The second hypothesis** is tested with the help of the following two parameters: (i) Capital Formation and (ii) Increase in the Investment in Plant & Machinery.

9. CAPITAL FORMATION

In this section the change in the capital formation, total of changes in the net fixed assets and the inventory, is compared between the years Y_o and Y_n. This comparison reveals the fact that whether the units have increased their capital formation from the year of takeover to the year for which latest financial data are available. Table - 4.21 presents a picture of the changes

Table - 4.21: Capital Formation in the Sample Units

(Rs. in lakh)

	Companies \ Years	Y_o	Y_n	Change	Capital Formation
1.	Dempo Dairy:				
	Fixed Assets	223.00	157.00	-66.00	-8.00
	Inventory	18.00	76.00	58.00	
2.	ICML:				
	Fixed Assets	72.62	68.16	-4.46	120.03
	Inventory	19.25	143.74	124.49	
3.	Amar Dye-Chem:				
	Fixed Assets	1,297.04	989.86	-307.18	-919.32
	Inventory	1,717.42	1,105.28	-612.14	
4.	Bokiyu Tanneries:				
	Fixed Assets	20.87	381.69	360.82	790.98
	Inventory	40. 63	470.79	430.16	
5.	India Precision:				
	Fixed Assets	652.18	862.64	210.46	435.51
	Inventory	199.37	424.42	225.05	
6.	Coramandal Pharma:				
	Fixed Assets	98.39	374.32	275.93	291.15
	Inventory	0. 22	15.44	15.22	
7.	Mico Farm Chemicals:				
	Fixed Assets	115.19	196.33	81.14	188.83
	Inventory	106.07	213.76	107.69	
8.	Sivamani Spinning:				
	Fixed Assets	228.83+	97.30	-131.53	-24.06
	Inventory	4.97	112.44	107.47	

Note: '+' indicates data for year Y_{-2}, as the data for Y_0 was not available.

in capital formation of the sample companies between the years Y_0 and Y_n.

Of the 8 units in the Table - 4.21, five units had a positive capital formation. The remaining three units had reduced their capital formation from year Y_o to Y_n. This implies that the following five companies have expanded their operations after the takeover:

1. ICML
2. Bokiyu Tanneries
3. India Precision
4. Mico Farm Chemicals, and
5. Coramandal Pharma

This in essence proves the hypothesis that after the takeover companies try to expand/modernise.

10. PLANT AND MACHINERY

Another parameter, which used to measure this hypothesis, is the increase in the investment in plant and machinery. An increase in the investment in this was a proof of the hypothesis. Table - 4.22 presents data of plant and machinery relating to the sample units for the years Y_o and Y_n.

Table - 4.22 : A Comparison of Plant and Machinery of Sample Units between the Years Y_o and Y_n

(Rs. in lakh)

Companies / *Years*	Y_o	Y_n	*Change*
Dempo Dairy	NA	NA	NA
ICML	22.07	33.77	11.70
Amar Dye-Chem	250.88	373.52	122.64
Bokiyu Tanneries	2.97	121.79	118.82
India Precision	811.00	568.25	-242.75
Coramandal Pharma	54.27	239.48	185.21
Mico Farm Chemicals	83.24	166.53	83.29
Sivamani Spinning	174.91+	54.13	120.78

Note: '+' indicates data for year Y_{-1}, as the data for year Y_o was not available.

Of the sample 8 units, data was not available for one unit and two units (India Precision and Sivamani Spinning) had showed a reduction in the investment in plant and machinery over this period and the remaining five had increased the size of investment in the plant and machinery.

To conclude, both the parameters proved the hypothesis that the companies, which had been taken over, shall try to expand in the process of turnaround.

11. FINDINGS

An attempt had been made in this chapter to study the impact of the takeover through the analysis of profitability of the sample companies. Profitability of the sample companies was analysed through various ratios and in terms of absolutes and decomposition analysis. During this study, a comparison was made between the year of the takeover (Y_0) and the latest year (Y_n) for which financial data were available with the companies. The results of the analysis are presented below:

1. As stated earlier, a company can be considered to have turned around in two situations: (1) If the company comes out from losses; and (2) If the company shows a declining trend of losses, in the post-takeover period.

Taking into consideration the **Gross Profits** of the companies under study, the following companies were able to convert gross losses into gross profits:

1. Dempo Dairy
2. ICML
3. India Precision
4. Mico Farm Chemicals
5. Sivamani Spinning

On the basis of **EBIT**, the following companies had positive EBITs and thereby turned around after the takeover:

1. Dempo Dairy

2. ICML
3. India Precision
4. Mico Farm Chemicals
5. Sivamani Spinning

Under this test also, Amar Dye-Chem and Bokiyu Tanneries were not successful. There had been increases and decreases in the negative EBIT of these two firms; whereas the Coramandal Pharma had an increasing negative EBIT.

The following companies had **operating profits** in the post-takeover period, i.e., they had converted their operating losses into operating profits:

1. Dempo Dairy
2. ICML
3. Mico Farm Chemicals
4. India Precision

Amar Dye-Chem and Bokiyu Tanneries did not show any trend with fluctuations from year to year. Coramandal Pharma had ever-increasing operating losses.

Sivamani Spinning had operating profit only in the year Y_3 and operating losses in the years Y_2 and Y_4.

On the basis of **Net Profit**, the following companies had a steady trend of net profits after the takeover:

1. Dempo Dairy
2. ICML
3. Bokiyu Tanneries
4. India Precision
5. Mico Farm Chemicals

India Precision, though had a net profit from year Y_1, there was a net loss in the year Y_3. The reason for this net loss had been explained earlier. The other two companies, i.e., Amar Dye-Chem and Coramandal Pharma had an ever-increasing net loss even after the takeover. Now, it could be concluded that these two companies could not respond to the turnaround efforts.

2. In case of ICML, though there had been profits after the takeover, they had been on a declining trend. This is a matter of serious concern. At this rate, the company might get into losses sooner or later. The declining rate at the operational level was faster than at net profit level. This means that the production related costs were on the increase and more particularly, the material costs are ever increasing. Hence, the company should be watchful and explore the ways and means of reducing these costs and thereby improve profits.

3. Among all the sample companies, Bokiyu Tanneries is a peculiar case. This has staged a turnaround with huge amounts of non-operating income. Of course, this includes a major proportion of income from job work. If one looks into the decomposition analysis of the total income, one could realise that there has been a change in the approach towards job work. In the initial years (Y_0,Y_1), there had been a high proportion of income from job work, followed by a mix of income from job work and operations in years Y_2 and Y_3 and finally, a major proportion of income from operations in years Y_4 and Y_5.

4. In case of Sivamani Spinning, it appears that the company has attempted turnaround and started improving its results upto year Y_3. Thereafter, in the year Y_4, there had been operating loss and net loss. It appeared from the statements of the people concerned with the company like Special Director and Financial Institutions that this declining trend has continued and the company had landed into financial problems. It was felt that all this has happened because of inefficient leadership even after the takeover.

5. It was evident from the study that turnaround efforts made by the changed management could not produce any results in the case of Coramandal Pharma.

6. Except in the case of Amar Dye-Chem, Bokiyu Tanneries and Coramandal Pharma, the cost of goods sold to sales was

less than a hundred per cent in all the years of the post-takeover period, which implied that these units were turning around after the takeover.

7. Except for Amar Dye-Chem and Coramandal Pharma, the proportion of Total Cost to Total Income was less than a hundred per cent in a majority of the years after the takeover, which was a sign of turnaround after the takeover.

8. In most of the companies, which had positive EBIT, the asset turnover was around 1 time in a majority of the years in the study period. It was less than 1 time for the companies, which had negative EBIT for many years. This phenomenon was supporting the Du Pont Analysis, which states that with increased asset turnover one should achieve a positive ROI even with low profit margins.

9. In the second part of this chapter, it is hypothesised that the companies that were taken over by the better known Management, turnaround faster than those that were taken over by the relatively lesser - known Managements. This hypothesis is verified by looking into the improvement in the variables such as liquidity, leverage, sales performance, net worth and total assets after the takeover. On the whole, the data could prove the hypothesis.

10. In order to prove the hypothesis pertaining to the expansion or modernisation after the takeover, the capital formation and investment in plant and machinery are used. On analysis, both these parameters have proved the hypothesis with a majority of sample units enhancing their capital formation and increasing their investment in plant and machinery during the post-takeover period.

REFERENCES

1. Duck, R.E.V. & Jervis, FR.J. (1964), *Management Accounting*, George G. Harrap & Company, p. 98.
2. N. P. Agarwal (1981), *Analysis of Financial Statements: A Case Study of Aluminium Industry in India*, National Publishing House, New Delhi.

3. Howard & Upton (1961), *Introduction to Business Finance,* McGraw Hill, New York, p. 150.
4. N.P. Agarwal, (1981), *op. cit.*
5. John, J. Hampton (1986), *Financial Decision-making: Concepts, Problems and Cases,* Prentice Hall of India Private Ltd, New Delhi.
6. Lawrence, B. Schall and Charles, W. Haley (1986), *Introduction to Financial Management,* McGraw Hill Book Company.
7. James C. Van Horne (1995), *Financial Management and Policy,* Prentice-Hall of India, New Delhi.
8. *ICICI Portfolio 1993-94* published by ICICI Ltd, Bombay.
9. *Reserve Bank of India Bulletin* (1994) Published by RBI Bombay.

Chapter V

SUMMARY OF FINDINGS AND SUGGESTIONS

1. THE STATEMENT OF THE PROBLEM

Takeover phenomenon, which swept the West during sixties and seventies, has come down to India during late eighties and the terms such as mergers, acquisitions and takeovers have turned out to be buzzwords today. With the adoption of liberalisation policies in the Indian economy in late eighties, the Indian corporate sector too started experiencing takeover activity.

The first wave of takeover activity in India can be said to have taken place between 1977 and 1985. During this period, the number of takeovers was few. With the liberalisation of provisions in the Industries (Development and Regulation) Act, 1951, and Monopolies and Restrictive Trade Practices Act, 1969, the second phase of takeover activity started in 1988, and there occurred 121 mergers and acquisitions during 1988-92. There has been a significant spurt in takeover activity since 1992. The game of takeover is now played by units of divergent character such as small and big, having low profile and high profile and of Indian and Foreign origin. As per the data available, it is estimated that about 1,000 mergers and takeovers have occurred between 1992 and 1995.

Though the takeover phenomenon is sweeping across India in 90's, there are no scientific studies done on the performance evaluation of the takeover units except few newspaper writings. Though a few researchers have concentrated on the takeover activity, they focused much on the motives and the capital market related matters. Little is done from the point of view of establishing the fact that whether takeovers are able to produce results and thus the Government and others can support them as a useful economic activity. More so, in the context of turning around of sick units, takeover is considered to be a useful strategy. In this context, the present study aims to concentrate on the aspects relating to performance of the units being takeover by the new managements. Sample selection is made from only sick companies for the sole reason that these changes in these units can be clearly identified. Hence, the study is based on the Board for Industrial and Financial Reconstruction (BIFR) cases, for the selection of the sample, which have undergone management change (takeover) as a strategy for the revival (turnaround).

Under the Sick Industrial Companies Act, 1985, (SICA) it is mandatory for a sick unit to report to the BIFR for its winding-up or for rehabilitation. As far as possible, the BIFR tries to rehabilitate a sick unit rather than winding it up. Generally, rehabilitation is done in the following ways:

1. Financial reconstruction of the company.
2. The amalgamation of the sick company with any other company or any other company with the sick company.
3. Sale or lease of a part or whole of any industrial unit of the sick company.
4. Proper management of the sick industrial company by change in or takeover of management of the sick company.

The BIFR after considering all the factors and the feelings of all the stakeholders, may sanction any one of the above methods in order to turn the company around.

For the present study, it is proposed to study the companies, which have been recommended by the BIFR for change of management or takeover, by a new management as a turnaround strategy. The study includes a comparision of the performance of these sick units during the pre and post-takeover periods from the points of view of *liquidity, leverage* and *profitability*.

2. OBJECTIVES OF THE STUDY

The main objective of the present study is to verify whether the takeovers had turned the companies around or not. More specifically, the study deals with the following:

1. To probe into whether the liquidity of the companies has improved with the takeover.
2. To study the effect of leverage on liquidity and on profitability and its changes over the study period.
3. To examine whether the takeover is leading the companies from losses to profits, as expected with the takeover.
4. To verify whether the taking over companies with better and proven management skills are able to bring about better and faster results.
5. To understand whether the companies selected for study are able to expand their activities after the takeover.

3. HYPOTHESES

In the light of the objectives described above, the following hypotheses are intended to be tested for their acceptance or non-acceptance:

1. The company should turnaround and achieve better liquidity, particularly the short-term liquidity after the takeover.
2. The capital structure of the taken over company should change in such a way that it should result in better solvency, liquidity and profitability.

3. When a company has been taken over by the new management, the company should turnaround and the profitability should improve.
4. The companies those were taken over by the better-known industrial groups, who have proven abilities of managing, shall turnaround faster than those that were taken over by the relatively lesser-known groups or individuals.
5. When a takeover of a sick unit takes place, the taken over company with the support of the taking over company shall try to expand or modernise their business activities in the process of their turning around.

FINDINGS

The following is the summary of the major findings emerged from this study:

4. LIQUIDITY ANALYSIS

The study started with a hypothesis that there is an improvement in the liquidity position of the sample units after the takeover. The hypothesis is verified with the help of certain standard ratios and funds flow analysis. The findings against the stated hypothesis are as follows:

1. All the companies except Amar Dye-Chem had better current ratios in the post-takeover period, when a comparision is made between the post and the pre-takeover periods. Amar Dye-Chem had more than 1:1 ratio before the takeover and it had been sharply declining in the post-takeover period. This implies that the company is gradually losing its liquidity. Though there is an improvement in the liquidity position after the takeover, most of the companies could not maintain the ideal ratio of 2:1.

2. As far as quick ratio is concerned, the sample companies are showing three types of trends. They are:

a. Companies with increasing quick ratio after the takeover,

b. Companies with a mixed trend i.e. some times increasing and sometimes decreasing quick ratio in the post-takeover, and

c. Companies with declining quick ratio.

Generally, all the companies had a better quick ratio in the post-takeover period. On the whole, only 6 out of the 8 companies have an ideal quick ratio of 1:1 in at least one or more of the years of study.

3. Absolute liquid assets are at nominal levels in almost all the companies even after the takeover.

4. There had been mostly negative net working capital in all the companies before the takeover. However, all the companies except Amar Dye-Chem, and Sivamani Spinning have registered positive net working capital during the post-takeover period. Going by the criteria of current ratio, quick ratio, and net working capital, the same six units proved to be more liquid after the takeover.

5. Going by the criteria of cash flows, except Amar Dye-Chem, all the sample companies have negative net cash flows in the pre-takeover period. Of these, all the companies (excepting Coramandal Pharma) have turned around .

Six companies had more current assets than the current liabilities and the excess poıtion of current assets had been financed by the long-term sources. These companies are:

1. Dempo Dairy
2. ICML
3. Bokiyu Tanneries
4. India Precision
5. Coramandal Pharma
6. Mico Farm Chemicals

The remaining two companies have used short-term funds for long-term uses and thereby diverted the funds for purposes other than those for which they had been raised.

1. Amar Dye-Chem
2. Sivamani Spg & Wng

It may be noticed from the above discussion that both methods have shown the same conclusions and thereby verified the funds figures and their sources and uses.

In the case of the following units there has been an increase in net working capital or current asset.

1. Dempo Dairy
2. ICML
3. Bokiyu Tanneries
4. India Precision
5. Coramandal Pharma
6. Mico Farm Chemicals

However, in the case of units below, there has been a further increase in the current liabilities.

1. Amar Dye-Chem
2. Sivamani Spinning

6. The structural analysis of the assets and liabilities with the help of decomposition technique reveals the dominant role of current assets in the asset structure of sample units. Among the current assets, inventory and receivables occupied high proportions. Similarly, the proportion of current liabilities to total debt has been on an increasing trend.

7. The analysis of sources and uses of funds has lead to the conclusion that, in a majority of the sample units, long-term funds have been used for short-term purposes. Interestingly, increase in the net worth of the companies had been a constant source of funds in a majority of the companies in the post-takeover period.

8. In the preceding sections, we have calculated net working capital figures and sources and uses of funds. Here, an attempt is made to study the changes of net working capital from the year of takeover to the year for which the accounting information is available say Y_n (as this keeps changing from company to company). This is compared with the changes (uses) of short-term funds, which have been calculated in sources and uses statement, subsequently. Finally, an attempt has been made to study the sources of short-term funds and their diversion, if any. The following table presents the changes of net working capital between Y_o and Y_n.

(Rs. in lakhs)

S.No.	*Name of the Company*	*Yo*	*Yn*	*Change*
1.	Dempo Dairy	-20.00	144.00	164.00
2.	ICML	-163.26	384.98	548.24
3.	Amar Dye-Chem	-446.33	-2963.37	-2517.04
4.	Bokiyu Tanneries	-135.53	187.14	322.67
5.	India Precision	-7.65	410.12	-417.77
6.	Coramandal Pharma	-104.32	24.76	129.08
7.	Mico Farm Chemicals	134.85	304.72	169.87
8.	Sivamani Spinning	-54.40	-79.99	-19.59

9. Going by the principle that a portion or permanent portion of working capital (short-term funds) has to be financed through permanent or long-term sources of funds for better liquidity, it may be concluded that the following units have better liquidity when a comparision is made between the year of takeover (Y_o) and the latest year for which financial data has been made available (Y_n).

1. Dempo Dairy
2. ICML

3. Bokiyu Tanneries
4. India Precision Bearing
5. Coramandal Pharma
6. Mico Farm Chemicals

The following are the companies, which had lost their liquidity from year Y_o to year Y_n.

1. Amar Dye-Chem
2. Sivamani Spinning

It may be concluded that the above companies are using short-term funds for long-term uses. This is happening because of the reason that the companies are not able to raise funds from long-term sources. When this kind of diversion takes place there is every likelihood of illiquidity.

5. LEVERAGE ANALYSIS

An attempt has been made to study the leverage of the sample units and its impact on solvency, liquidity and profitability with particular reference to the improvement or otherwise, recorded by the units taken up for the study. Such an attempt has lead us to the following major conclusions:

1. When an attempt is made to measure the leverage through usual techniques, it was found to be erroneous and unreliable as the figures used for such an exercise turned out to be negative for a majority of the years in the sample units. As such the study depended on the analysis of leverage through certain ratios suggested in the finance literature.

2. Studied thus, the debt-equity ratio, one of the important indicators of leverage, had increased in the very first year of takeover (Y_0) in the following units. That is to say, the equity of these companies was more or less static and the debt finance had been used for the needs of turnaround. The companies are:

1. Dempo Dairy

2. Bokiyu Tanneries
3. India Precision Bearings, and
4. Mico Farm Chemicals

Mico Farm Chemicals, had increased their equity only in the year Y_2. This is why the debt-equity ratio of this company had started declining from year Y_2. The remaining companies had brought additional equity capital to meet the turnaround needs in the initial years of takeover itself, (Y_o or Y_1). However, there are many changes in the subsequent years of takeover. These changes are mainly due to changes in the debt in most of the sample companies.

3. The following companies enhanced the equity for the purposes of implementing turnaround after pattern of financing takeover. The companies are:

1. ICML
2. Amar Dye-Chem
3. Coramandal Pharma
4. Sivamani Spinning

Coramandal Pharma had increased its equity capital in almost every year after the takeover.

4. The study revealed the fact that in most of the sample units, total debt was in excess of the total assets even after the takeover. Consequently, the creditors are at a greater risk, as the assets are not sufficient to meet their loan obligations. Though, there had been a general decline in the proportion of total debt to total assets in most of the sample units, only three companies, viz. Bokiyu Tanneries, Coramandal Pharma and Mico Farm Chemicals, had a ratio of less than one time in the year Y_n. This implies that the creditors in these three companies are secure as the total assets are in excess of the total debt.

5. In the present study, most of the companies had low equity compared total assets. Equity capital as a percentage of total assets was varying between the lowest of 2 per cent and

the highest of 87 per cent. Further, there was a declining trend in the proportion of equity to total assets among the sample units.

6. Normally, in a healthy unit, the total assets are financed by the equity, debt and retained earnings. Therefore, the total of assets will always be more than the total of equity and debt put together. In this study, the total assets are always less than a hundred per cent in the pre-takeover period. However, the situation has gradually improved over the post-takeover period in a majority of the units. Hence, it could be concluded that after the takeover the accumulated losses have gradually declined and there were reserves and surpluses in some cases, thus implying turnaround.

7. The ratio of EBITD to total debt has been positive in most of the sample units after the takeover. Out of the eight units selected for the study there were two units, which had an ever-increasing ratio, four companies had a mixed trend with frequent increases and decreases and the remaining two companies had no positive ratio. This indicates that only the last two units have failed to turnaround even with the new management from the point of view of liquidity. Even the ratio of EBITD to long-term debt was showing more or less similar trend.

8. The ratio of Total Debt and Equity to Earnings Before Interest Taxes and Depreciation reveals the extent of earnings available to cover the debt and equity obligations at a given point of time. Usually, a ratio of more than 8 times is said to be an alarming level. In the present analysis five units are having a ratio of less than 8 times in at least one of the years after the takeover. Thus implying that these units have turned around and the proportion of earnings have improved thereby resulting in decline in this ratio. The remaining 3 units never had a ratio of less than 8 times even after the takeover.

9. Since, all units selected for study are sick units and are in the process of turnaround. Naturally, the EBIT of these units would have been negative before the takeover and in case of

some it would have become positive after the takeover. Therefore, it could be possible to calculate the interest coverage ratios of only these companies. In this category, there are only five companies out of the eight selected for the study. Since, there are better interest coverage ratios in these companies after the takeover, it may be concluded that these companies have turned around.

10. Since, the proportion of interest to EBIT has not revealed much insights, it was decided to compare the interest charges with the total income. As a general rule, the interest burden increases when the debt burden increases and when the debt increases it should normally go into productive use and should help in increasing the total income. This need not be always true in the case of sick units. It is found that all the sample units (except Coramandal Pharma) have declining proportions of interest to total income after takeover. Normally, this kind of decline occurs in three situations as evident from the analysis : (a) a decreasing interest burden with stable total income or (b) an increasing total income with stable interest charges or (c) both a decrease in the interest burden and an increase in the total income. Because of one of the above reasons the proportion had been declining after the takeover.

11. Interest as a percentage of gross profits reveals the ability of the firm to meet the interest obligation of a unit from the gross profit. In the present study, it was found that five out of eight units had gross profits in the post-takeover period. This ratio was showing a mixed trend in four out of these five units, even in the post-takeover period and the remaining one unit is continuously declining. However, all these five units have positive gross profit figures. Thus, these units are considered to be units where the efforts of turnaround had worked well.

12. On analysing the pattern of financing the assets of these sample units, it is found that five of the eight units could reduce their accumulated losses and were able to register improvement after the takeover. Among these five units, two units were able to wipe out their accumulated losses completely and registered surpluses. The remaining three of the sample eight units had

increased their accumulated losses even after the takeover. These three units had used up a portion of funds those would have normally been used for financing assets and thereby could not turnaround even after the takeover.

6. PROFITABILITY ANALYSIS

The results of the analysis of profitability are presented below:

1. As regards profitability, a company can be considered to have turned around in two situations: (1) if the company comes out from losses; and (2) if the company shows a declining trend of losses, in the post-takeover period.

Taking into consideration the Gross Profits of the companies under study, the following companies have traveled from gross losses to gross profits:

1. Dempo Dairy
2. ICML
3. India Precision
4. Mico Farm Chemicals
5. Sivamani Spinning

Among the remaining companies under study, Amar Dye-Chem and Bokiyu Tanneries are not showing any trend. There had been increases and decreases in the net losses of these units. Coramandal Pharma had increasing gross losses even in the post-takeover period. On the basis of the Earnings Before Interest and Taxes (EBIT) the following companies have positive EBITs and thereby have turned around after the takeover:

1. Dempo Dairy
2. ICML
3. India Precision
4. Mico Farm Chemicals
5. Sivamani Spinning

Under this test also, Amar Dye-Chem and Bokiyu Tanneries were not successful. There had been increases and decreases in the negative EBIT of these two firms, whereas the Coramandal Pharma had an increasing negative EBIT.

The following companies have operating profits in the post-takeover period i.e. they have converted their operating losses into operating profits. This shift could be in the year Y_1 or Y_2 or even in Y_3 or even in subsequent years.

1. Dempo Dairy
2. ICML
3. Mico Farm Chemicals
4. India Precision

Dempo Dairy started its turnaround in relation to operating profit only in the year Y_2 and continued afterwards also. Mico Farm Chemicals travelled from operating loss to operating profit only in the year Y_4. India precision has turn around in the year Y_1 with a declining operating loss and showed an operating profit in the year Y_2. It showed an operating loss again in the year Y_3 and became positive in the year Y_4 and the positive trend continued in year Y_5 and Y_6 also.

Amar Dye-Chem and Bokiyu Tanneries did not show any trend with fluctuations from year to year. Coramandal pharma has ever-increasing operating losses. Sivamani Spinning had operating profit only in the year Y_3 and operating losses in the years Y_2 and Y_4. The reason for this is increasing costs of good sold.

On the basis of **Net Profit,** the following companies have a steady trend of net profits after the takeover.

1. Dempo Dairy
2. ICML
3. Bokiyu Tanneries
4. India Precision
5. Mico Farm Chemicals

India Precision, though has a Net Profit from year Y_1, there was a net loss in the year Y_3. The reason for this net loss has been explained earlier. The other two companies i.e. Amar Dye-Chem and Coramandal Pharma have an ever-increasing net loss even after the takeover. Now, it can be concluded that these two companies could not respond to the turnaround efforts, those were initiated after the takeover. An interesting observation here is that the Bokiyu Tanneries has joined in the list of companies, which have turned around, only at the net profit level with a continuous stream of net profits. It may be recalled that this company had always-gross losses, negative EBIT and even operating losses. This interesting change has happened because of the presence of huge amounts of non-operating incomes, which includes huge amounts of income from job work also.

Similarly, in the case of Sivamani Spinning, though there were operating losses in the years Y_2 and Y_4, there was net profit in the year Y_2 and a reduced net loss in the year Y_4. This is because of the presence of non-operating income, as explained earlier.

2. In case of ICML, though there had been profits after the takeover, they were on a declining trend. This is a matter of serious concern. At this rate, the company may get into losses sooner or later. The declining rate at the operational level is faster than at net profit level. This means that the production related costs are on the increase and more particularly, the material costs are ever increasing. Hence, the company should be watchful and explore the ways and means of reducing these costs and thereby improve profits.

3. Among all the sample companies, Bokiyu Tanneries is a peculiar case. This has staged a turnaround with huge amounts of non-operating income. Of course, this includes a major proportion of income from job work. If one looks into the the decomposition analysis of the total income one can realise that there has been a strategic change in the approach towards job work. In the initial years (Y_0, Y_1), there had been a high proportion of income from job work, followed by a mix of

income from job work and operations in years Y_2 and Y_3 and finally, a major proportion of income from operations in years Y_4 and Y_5. This strategic change can be seen very clearly.

4. In case of Sivamani Spinning, it appears that the company had attempted turnaround and started improving its results upto year Y_3. Thereafter, in the year Y_4, there had been operating loss and net loss. It appears from the statements of the people concerned with the company like Special Director and Financial Institutions, that this declining trend continued and the company landed in financial problems. It is felt that all this had happened because of inefficient leadership even after the takeover.

5.It is evident from the study that turnaround efforts made by the changed management could not produce any results in the case of Coramandal Pharma.

6. Except in the case of Amar Dye-Chem, Bokiyu Tanneries and Coramandal Pharma, the cost of goods sold to sales is less than a hundred per cent in all the years of the post-takeover period, which implies that these units are turning around after the takeover.

7. Except for Amar Dye-Chem and Coramandal Pharma the proportion of Total Cost to Total Income is less than a hundred per cent in a majority of the years after the takeover, which is a sign of turnaround after the takeover.

8. In most of the companies, which have the positive EBIT, the asset turnover was around 1 time in a majority of the years of the study period. It is less than 1 time for the companies, which had the negative EBIT. This corroborates with the principle underlying the Du Pont Analysis, which says that the increased asset turnover can achieve a positive ROI even with low profit margins.

SUGGESTIONS

An attempt is made in this section to make some suggestions for implementation by the sample units, operating agencies and the Government.

7. SUGGESTIONS TO THE SAMPLE UNITS

Since the study mainly focuses on the performance of the sample units, the units are advised to concentrate on the following issues for achieving better performance:

1. Though there is an improvement in the liquidity position after the takeover, most of the companies could not maintain the ideal ratio of 2:1. Moreover there is no consistency in the performance of the units over a period of time, emphasising the scope for further improvement. The sample companies are required to focus particularly on the management of cash flows and diversion of short-term fund for long-term uses. It is observed from the study that the percentage of the non-operating income is found to be significant in the sample units. A glaring example in this context is Bokiyu Tanneries. For the long-term survival of the companies, it is better that they concentrate more on the generation of operating income through the main business activity.

2. It appears from the study that the companies are highly levered. Total debt is found to be in excess of total assets even after the takeover. Consequently the creditors are at a greater risk. As a matter of fact, the debt equity proportions in the Indian Corporate Sector is only 1:1 compared to the 4:1 positions prevailing in the sample units. Unless the firms concentrate on reducing the debt proportion, there is every danger of the firms becoming defaulters in their payments. There is a need to introduce fresh equity capital to tide over the situation. The Managements of the taken-over companies should bring in the additional capital in the form of equity rather than in the form of debt.

3. Though there are net profits in many cases after the takeover, their proportion to sales was quite less. Therefore, the sample units should improve their profit margin either by increasing the operational efficiency

or by enhancing prices of finished products as the case may be.

8. SUGGESTIONS TO THE OPERATING AGENCIES (OAs)

As per the provisions of the SICA, the OA is required to prepare the rehabilitation scheme and submit the same to the BIFR. Though Financial Institutions and Commercial Banks are preparing the rehabilitation schemes, not all of them have the requisite facilities and competency for preparing a sound proposal. As a result of this, the proposals are not reflecting the true position and projections of the units involved. Therefore, there is a need to set up a specialised cell for carrying out this job.

Further, the Operating Agencies should play a sincere and committed role in turning around a company. In practice, these Operating Agencies are preparing rehabilitation schemes and are financing them. But there is no proper and continuous monitoring after the takeover. The primary responsibility of the turning around a sick company should primarily be the responsibility of Operating Agencies and they should be in continuous touch with the BIFR for remedial actions.

9. SUGGESTIONS TO THE GOVERNMENT

These suggestions are categorised under two headings:

1. Suggestions in relation to the strengthening of the BIFR, and
2. Suggestions for making/amending the required legislation.

9.1. Suggestions for improving the BIFR

In order to strengthen the hands of the BIFR the Government can think of the following measures:

1. One common criticism against the BIFR process is that it is a time consuming process and it takes a lot of time to get the rehabilitation scheme sanctioned. Naturally,

this delay results in the escalation of costs and force units in many cases to die. It is, therefore, necessary to revamp the functioning of the BIFR by strengthening its structure. The BIFR process must be time-bound and the whole process of rehabilitation of a sick company should be completed within, say, 3 or 6 months from filling of the case.

2. In order to make the BIFR a competent and effective body, its composition needs to be strengthened by appointing members who are experts in different fields like, Industry, Finance, Taxation, Law, Labour Matters, Accountancy, Marketing, Technology, etc. There is already a provision in the SICA for appointment of members. However, this has not been implemented. Most of the present members are Civil Servants.

3. The BIFR needs to be decentralised by establishing its offices at different parts of the country. This would enable better monitoring of the sanctioned schemes. At present monitoring is not done properly. There is every need to appoint proper experts for monitoring work rather than leaving it to Section Officers and Clerical Staff. These monitoring experts should do the monitoring regularly and bring the discrepancies and deviations to the notice of the Board Members for appropriate action.

4. The BIFR is a quasi - judicial body and, therefore, it is only recommendatory authority. In order to deal with the problem of sickness effectively, the BIFR should be given mandatory powers, so that it could order the agencies concerned to implement the rehabilitation package in ***totto*** and within the prescribed time limit.

5. As on today there are several Acts which are governing the takeover activity in India. Therefore, there is a need for a set of rules governing the takeovers. A single monitoring authority whose decisions could be appealed against a high-powered Tribunal must

govern the takeovers. The tribunal should take the place of the high courts and all other judicial authorities, except perhaps the Supreme Court.

9.2. Suggestions for Suitable Legislation

Since, the takeovers are centered on the tax benefits offered by the Government, the latter could consider the following for implementation:

1. As the tax benefit under Sec. 72(A) of the Income Tax Act, as one of the primary motivators of the takeover of sick companies, the Government should give back this power to the BIFR in order to facilitate this process.
2. The BIFR should also be empowered to permit the company to carry back business losses suffered by them and set those off as far as possible against the profits assessed to tax in the lost 3 or 4 years, as is in vogue in countries like the U.S.
3. The capital gains on sale of property by the sick units should be exempted from the tax, if these are invested into the rehabilitation process of the sick units.

BIBLIOGRAPHY

BOOKS

1. Agarwal, H.P. (1981), *Analysis of Financial Statements: A Case Study of Aluminium Industry in India*, National Publishing House, New Delhi.
2. Archer, S.H. and D'Ambrosio, C.A. (1972), *Business Finance—Theory and Management*, The MacMillan Company, New York.
3. Ashok Kumar N. and Parchute, Rajas (1990), *Mergers and Takeovers in India*, The Times Research Foundation, Pune.
4. Auerbach, Alan J. (Ed.) (1988), *Corporate Takeovers: Causes and Consequences*, University of Chicago Press, Chicago.
5. Butters, J.K., John Lintner, and W.L. Cary (1951), *Effect of Taxation on Corporate Mergers*, Harvard University Press, Cambridge, M.A.
6. Cooke, Terenece E. (1986), *Mergers and Acquisitions*, Basil Blackwell Ltd., Oxford.
7. Cowling, Keith, and et al. (1980), *Mergers and Economic Performance*, Cambridge University, London.
8. Dewing, Arther Stone (1914), *Corporate Promotions and Reorganisation*, Harvard University Press, Cambridge.
9. Gitman, L.J. (1976), *Principles of Management Finance*, Harper & Row, New York.
10. Goble, Devsa L., and White, Lawrence J., *A Time-Series*

Analysis of Mergers and Acquisitions in the U.S. Economy, Chapter 9 in Alan J. Auerbach, ed., 1988, *Corporate Takeover: Causes and Consequences*, The University of Chicago Press, Chicago.

11. Gort, Micheal (1962), *Diversification and Integration in American Industry*, Princeton University Press, Princeton.

12. Grene, Thomas L. (1897) *Corporation Finance*, Pitman, New York.

13. Gupta, L.C. and Sekhar, Archana, (1988), *Controlling Corporate Sickness: Lessons from Experiences for Managers and Bankers*, Oxford University Press.

14. Hampton, J.J. (1986), *Financial Decision Making: Concepts, Problems and Cases*, Prentice – Hall of India Pvt. Ltd., New Delhi.

15. Kaveri, V.S. (1986), *Financial Analysis of Company Mergers in India*, Himalaya Publishing House, Bombay.

16. Khan, M.Y., and Jain, P.K. (1992), *Financial Management: Text and Cases*, Tata McGraw Hill Publishing Company, New Delhi.

17. Kelly, E.M. (1967), *The Profitability of Growth through Merger*, Pennsylvania State University.

18. Kretal, N.R.A., and et al. (1969), *Mergers: A European Approach to Technique*, Business Books, London.

19. Markham, Jesse U. (1955), *Survey of Evidence and Findings on Mergers, Business Concentration and Price Policy*, Princeton University Press, Princeton, N.J., p. 156.

20. Mead, Edwards (1910), *Corporation Finance*, Appleton, New York.

21. Parashar, S.P. (1986), *Liquidity Management*, Vision Books, New Delhi.

22. Puliani, Ravi, and Puliani, Mahesh, Ed. (1995) *Sick Industrial Companies (Special Provisions) Act, 1985 and Board of Industrial and Financial Reconstruction Regulations, 1987*, Bharat Publications, Delhi.

23. Rao, K.V. (1990), *Management of Working Capital in Public Enterprises*, Deep & Deep Publications, Delhi.

24. Ravenscraft, David J., and Scherer, F.M. (1987), *Mergers, Self-offs and Economic Efficiency*, Brookings Institution, Washington, D.C.

25. Reid, Samuel R. (1968), *Mergers, Managers and the Economy*, McGraw-Hill, New York.

26. Roy, Malay K. (1989), *Takeovers: A Corporate Finance Approach*, Unpublished ICSSR Project Study.

27. Samuels, J.M., (Ed.) (1972), *Readings on Mergers and Takeovers*, Paul Elek Books Ltd., London.

28. Salter, Malcom S., and Wolf A. Weinhold (1980), *Merger Trends and Prospectives for the 1980*, US Department of Commerce, Harvard University, Dec., 80.

29. Shrivastava, Paul (1994), *Strategic Management Concepts and Practices*, South – Western Publishing Co., Ohio.

30. Singh, Ajit (1971), *Takeovers: Their Relevance to the Stock Market and Theory of the Firm*, Cambridge University Press, Cambridge.

31. Slatter, Stuart (1984), *Corporate Recovery: Successful Turnaround Strategies and their Implementation*, Penguin Books, Middlesex.

32. Stallworthy, E.A. and Kharbanda, O.P. (1988), *Takeovers, Acquisitions and Mergers: Strategies for Rescuing Companies in Distress*, Kogan Page, London.

33. Steiner, Peter O. (1977), *Mergers: Motives, Effects, Policies*, University of Michigan Press, Ann Arbor.

34. Stocking, G.W. (1955), *Commentary on Markham, Survey of Guidance and Findings on Mergers, in Business Concentration and Price Policy*, Princeton University Press, Princeton, N.J.

35. Van Horne, James C. (1995), *Financial Management and Policy*, Prentice-Hall of India Pvt. Ltd., New Delhi.

36. Verma, J.C. (1995), *Corporate Mergers, Amalgamations and Takeovers*, Bharat Publishing House, Delhi.

37. Weston, Fred J., Chung, Kwang S., and Hoag, Susan E. (1996) *Mergers, Restructuring and Corporate Control*, Prentice-Hall of India Pvt. Ltd., New Delhi.

38. FTC Report (1970), *Current Trends in Merger Activity*, Report No. 8, United States Government Printing Office, Washington D.C.

ARTICLES

1. Bharucha, M.P. (1996), "Takeovers Code and Implications," *Chartered Secretary*, March, 96.

2. Benston, G., and Sorter, G.H. (1960), "Appraising the Defensive Position of a Firm — The Internal Measure," *The Accounting Review*, 35 (6) October, 60.

3. Bierman, H. (1960), "Measuring Financial Liquidity," *The Accounting Review*, 30 (5) October, 60.

4. Binder, Denis (1973), "Securities Law of Contested Tender Offers," *New York Law Forum*, 16 (3) Winter, 73.

5. Boyle, Stanley (1970), "Pre-Merger Growth and Profit United States 1948-1968," *St. John's Law Review*, Special Edition, Spring, 70.

6. Franks, et al. (1976), "An Industry Study of the Profitability of Mergers," London School of Business Studies, Institute of Finance and Accounting *Discussion Paper*.

7. Gagon, J.M., et al. (1982), "Stock Market Behaviour of Merging Firms," *European Economic Review*, 17.

8. Gilbert, Frederick S., Jr. (1978), "Financing the Leverage buy-out through the Acquired Assets," *Harvard Business Review*, July-Aug., 78.

9. Gort, Thomas F. (1970), "New Evidence on Mergers," *Journal of Law and Economics* 13 (1).

10. Hagarty, Thomas P. (1970), "The Profitability of Corporate Mergers," *Journal of Business*, 43 (3) July, 70.

11. Halpern, P.J. (1973), "Empirical Estimates of the Amount and Distribution of Gains to Companies in Mergers," *Journal of Business*, 46.

12. Hamel, Gary and Prahalad C.K. (1994), Competing for the Futures," *Harvard Business Review*, July-Aug. 94.

13. Hayes Samuel L. III and Taussig, Russell A. (1967), "Tactics of Cash Takeover Bids," *Harvard Business Review*, 45 (2) March – April, 67.

14. Hector, Gary (1984), "Is Any Company Safe from Takeover," *Fortune*, April 2, 84.

15. Hindley, Brain (1970), "Separation of Ownership and Control in the Modern Corporation," *Journal of Law and Economics*, 13 (1).

16. Kanter, Rosabeth Mose (1974), "Collaborative Advantages: The Art Alliances," *Harvard Business Review*, July-Aug., 94.

17. Kitching, J. (1967), "Why do Mergers Miscarry?," *Harvard Business Review*, Nov-Dec., 67.

18. Lamke, K.V. (1970), "The Evaluation of Liquidity—An Analytical Study, *Journal of Accounting Research*, Spring, 70.

19. Lev. Baruch, and Mandelkar, Gershon (1972), "The Micro Economic Consequences Mergers," *Journal of Business*, 45 (1) Jan. 72.

20. Levinson, H. (1970), "A Psychologist Diagnosis Merger Failures," *Harvard Business Review*, March-April, 70.

21. Ninden, Cathy M. (1993), "An Empirical Examination of White Knight Corporate Takeovers: Synergy and Overbidding," *The Financing Management*, Winter, 93.

22. Payne, Adrian, F. (1987), "Approaching Acquisitions Strategically," *Journal of General Management*, 13(2) Winter, 87.

23. Rao, K.V., and Ravi Sankar, K. (1997), "Managerial Challenges in Corporate Takeovers in the Post-liberalisation Era," *The Management Accountant*, June, 97.

24. Salter, Malcom, S. and Weinhold, Wolf, A. (1978), "Diversification Via Acquisition: Creating Value," *Harvard Business Review*, July - Aug. 78.

25. Stingler, George J. (1950), "Monopoly and Oligopoly by Merger," *American Economic Review*, May, 50.

26. George J. (1951), "The Division of Labor is Limited by the Extent of the Market, *Journal of Political Economy*, June 1951.

27. Subramanian, S. (1996), "Evaluation of Strategies for Mergers, Amalgmations and Acquisitions," *The Management Accountant*, November, 96.

28. Vijaya Kumar, A. (1996), "Assessment of Corporate Liqiduity—A Discriminant Analysis Approach," The Management Accountant, Aug. 96.

29. Walter, James E. (1957), "Determination of Technical Solvency," *Journal of Business*, 30 (1), Jan., 57.

30. Wansley, James W., and et al. (1983), "Abnormal Returns to Acquired Firms by Type of Acquisition and Method of Payment, *The Financial Management*, Autumn, 83.

31. Weston, J. Fred. and Mansighka, Surendra K. (1971), "Tests of the Efficiency Performances of Conglomerate Firms," *Journal of Finances*, 26 (4) Sept. 71.

INDEX

❑❑❑